I F#cking Love Coloring!

AF351172

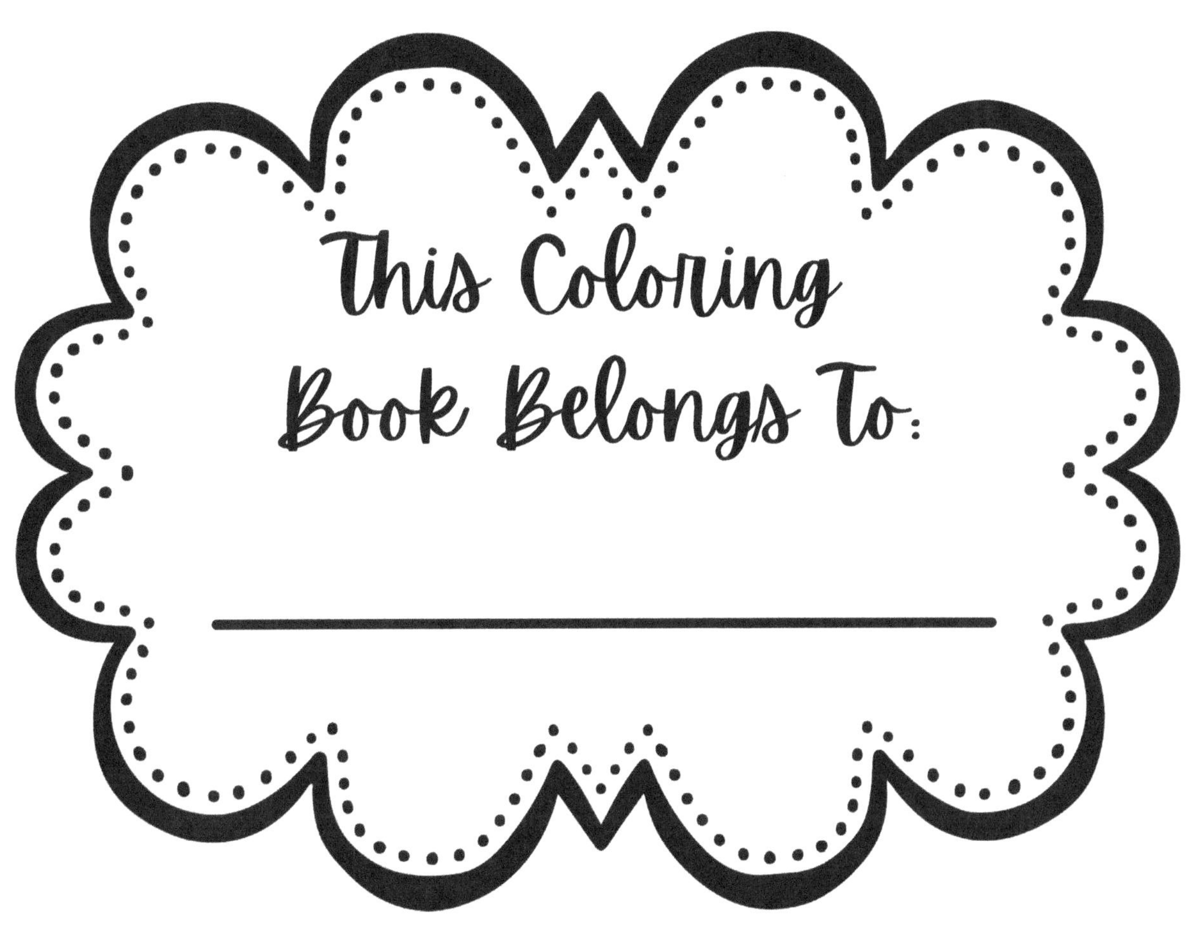

34 Relaxing Swear Word Coloring Pages For Adults

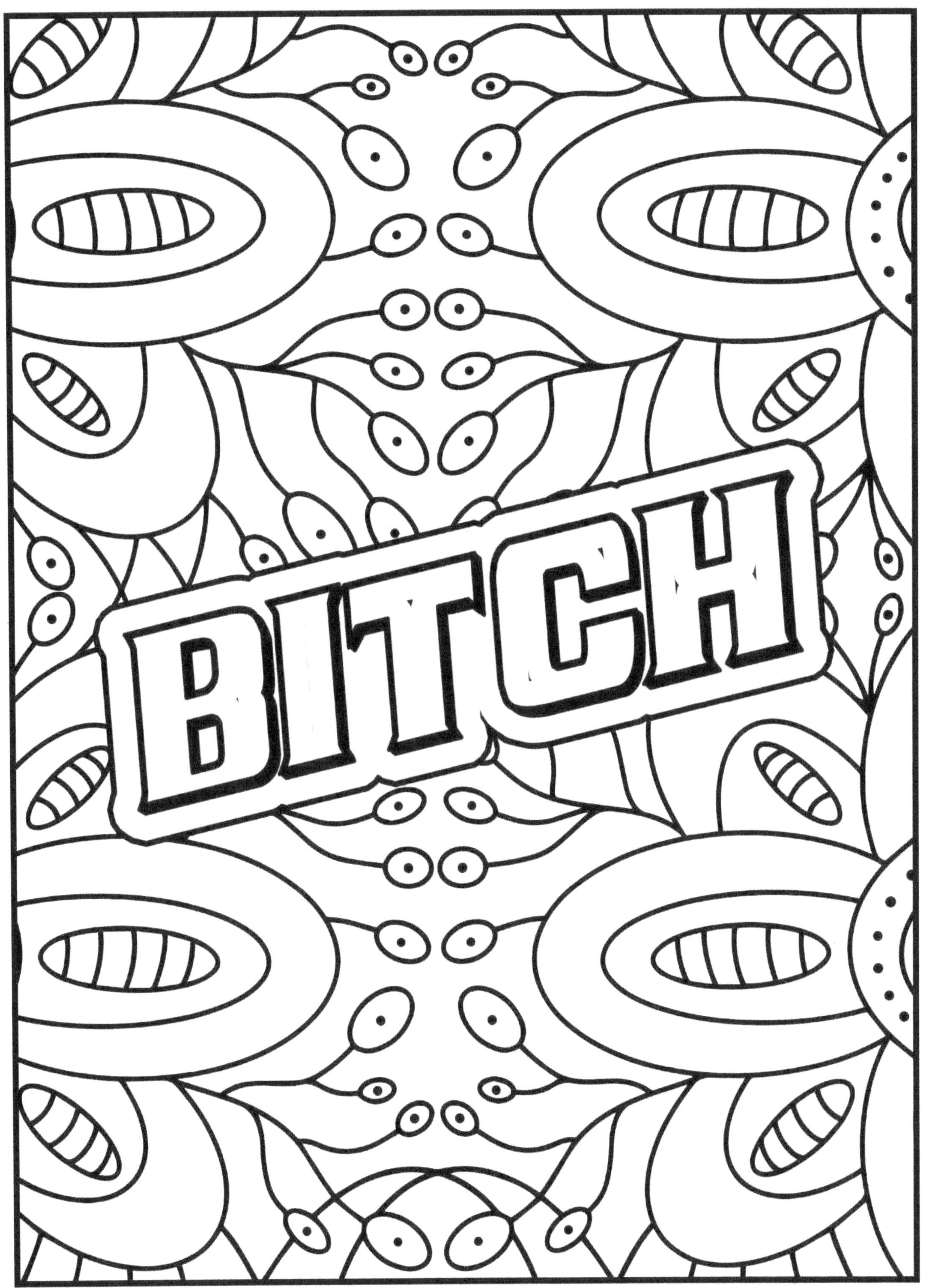
BITCH

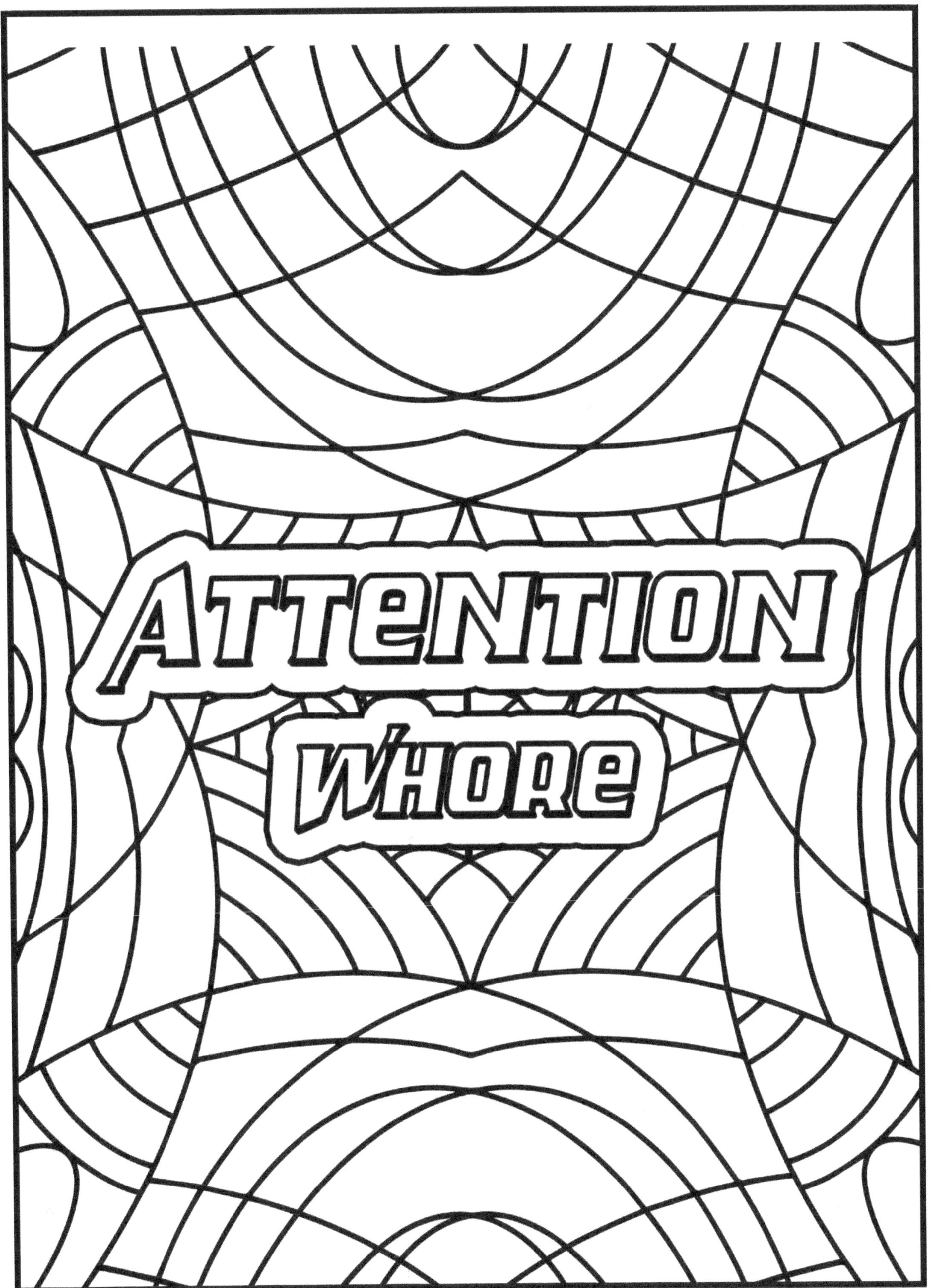

ATTENTION
WHORE

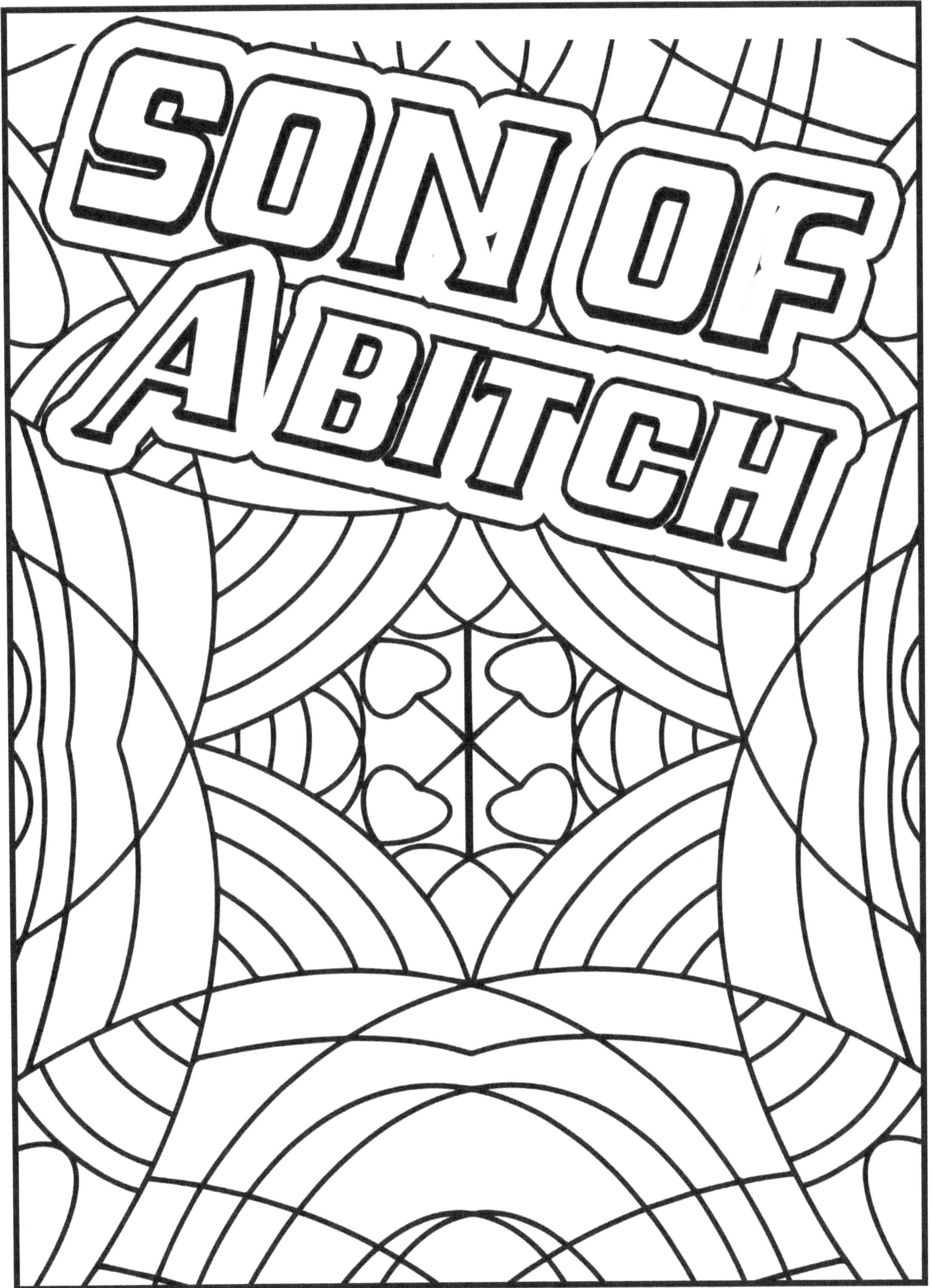
SON OF A BITCH

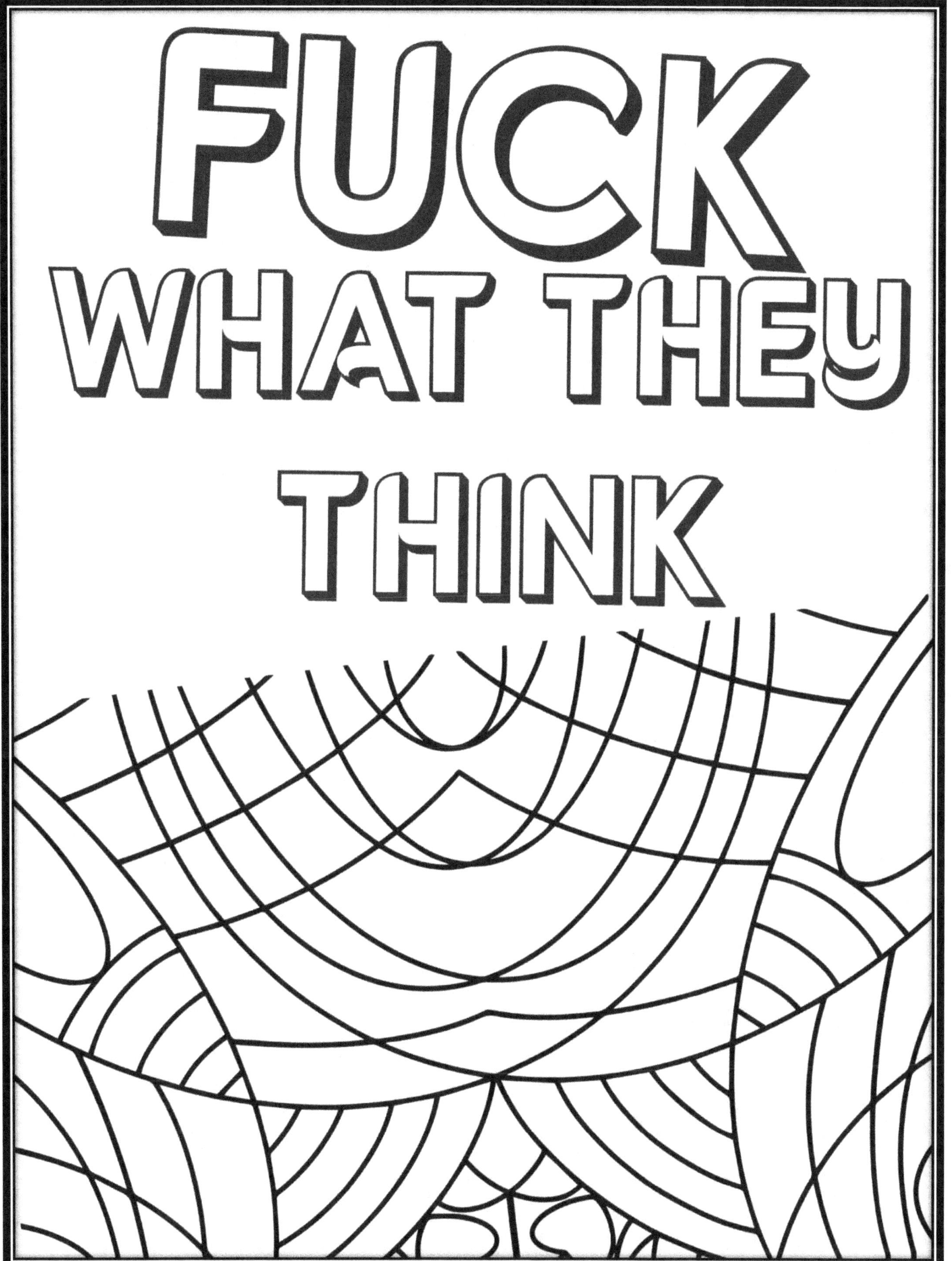

FUCK
WHAT THEY
THINK

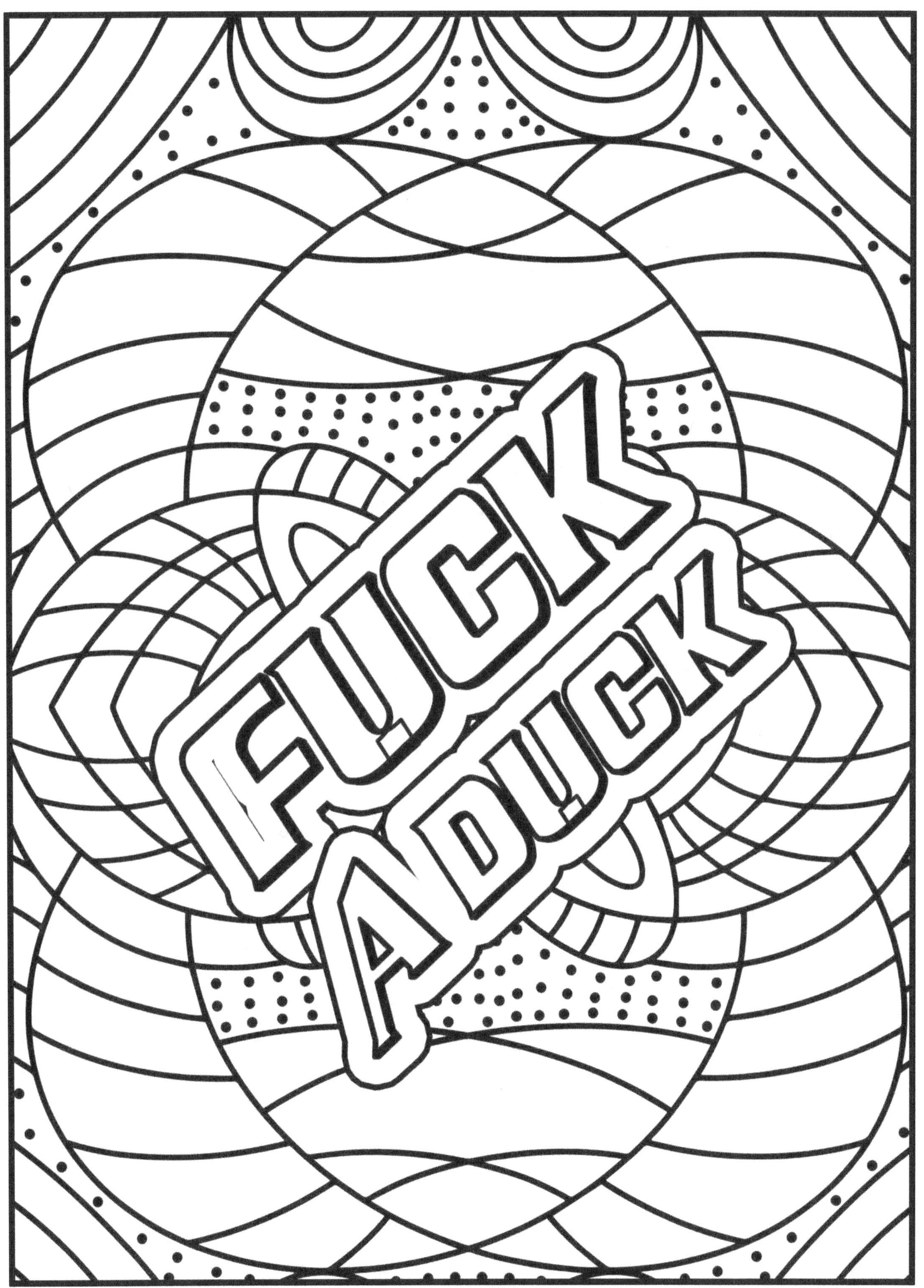

FUCK
A DUCK

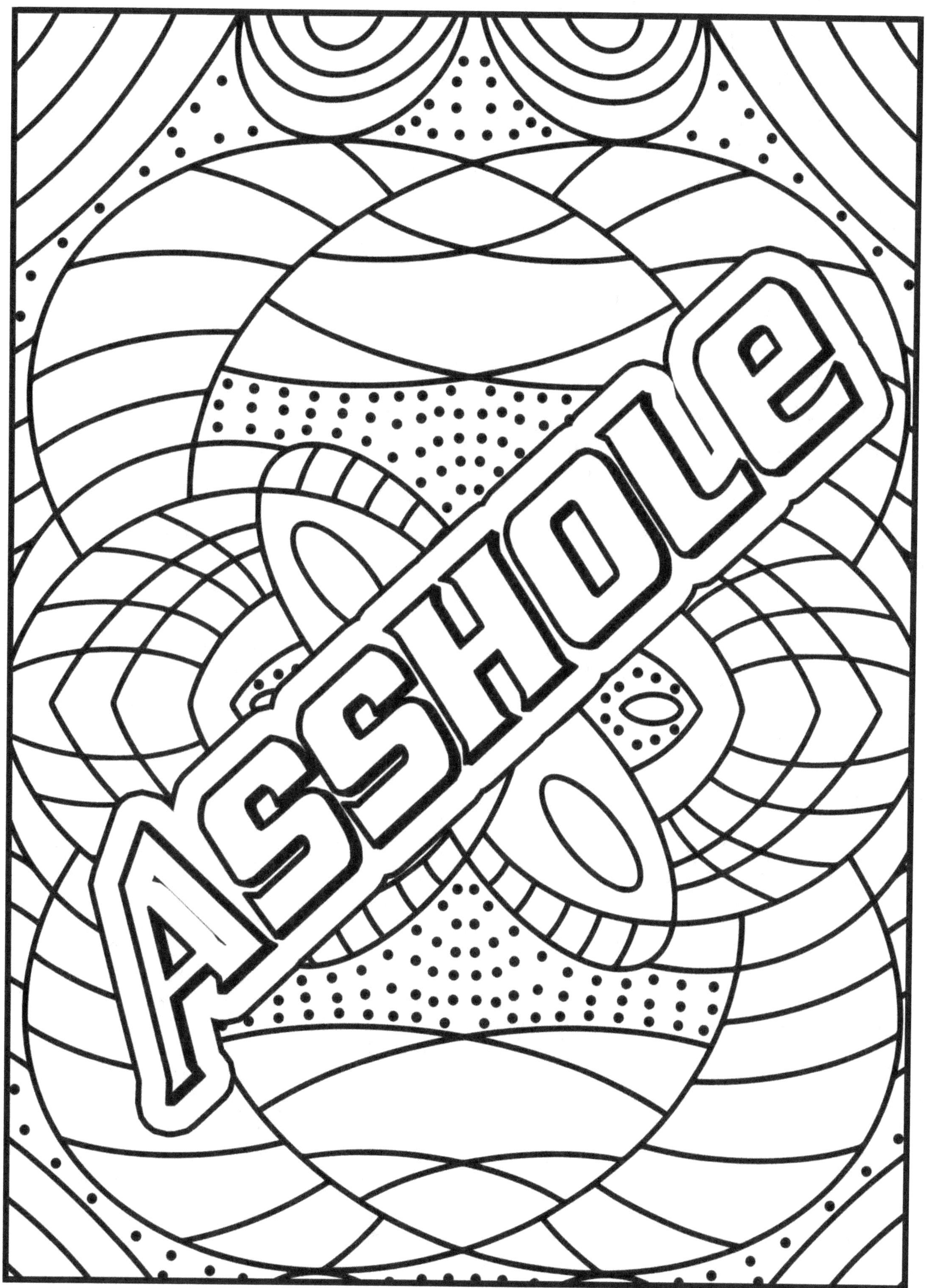

ASSHOLE

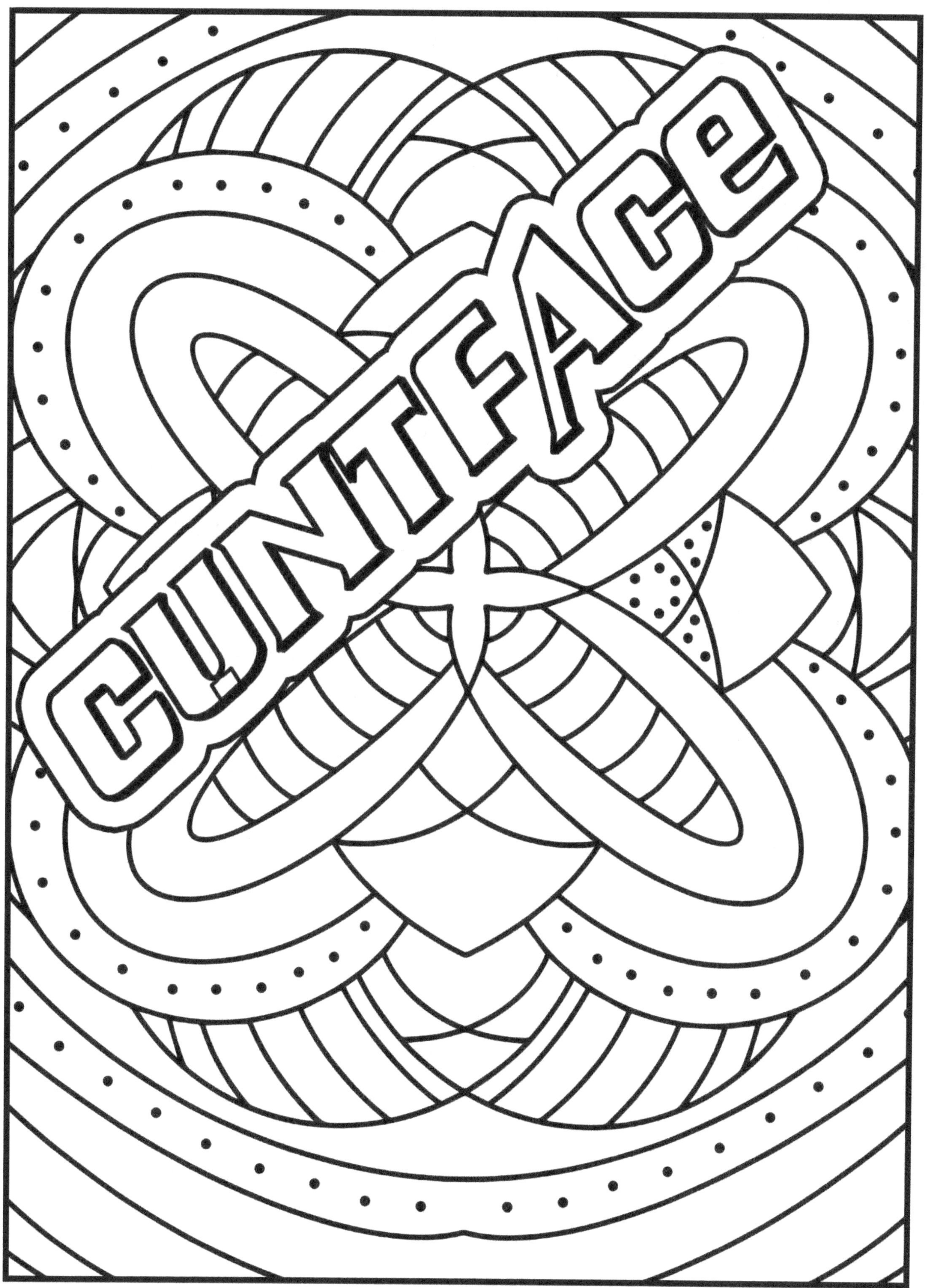
CUNTFACE

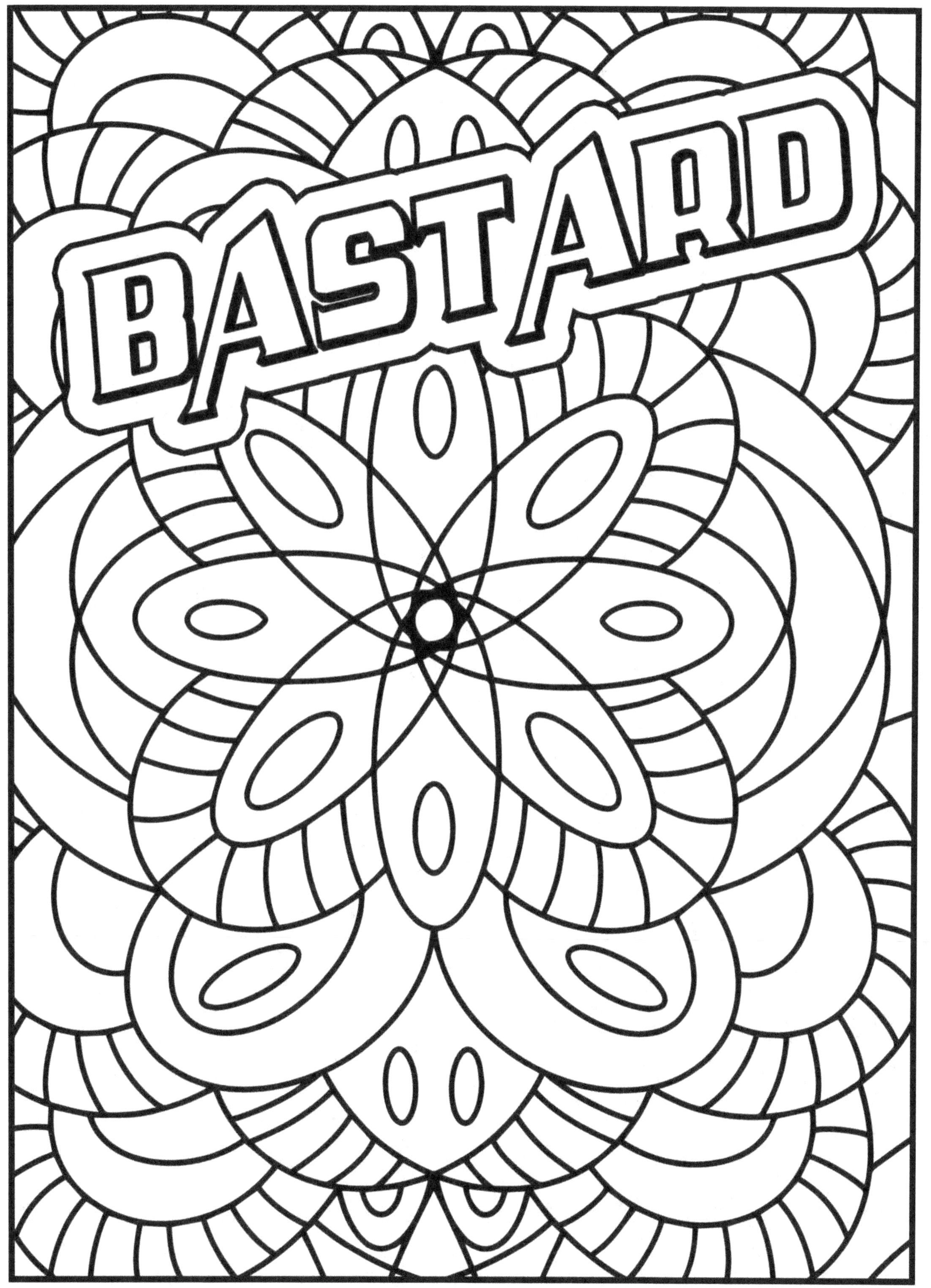
BASTARD

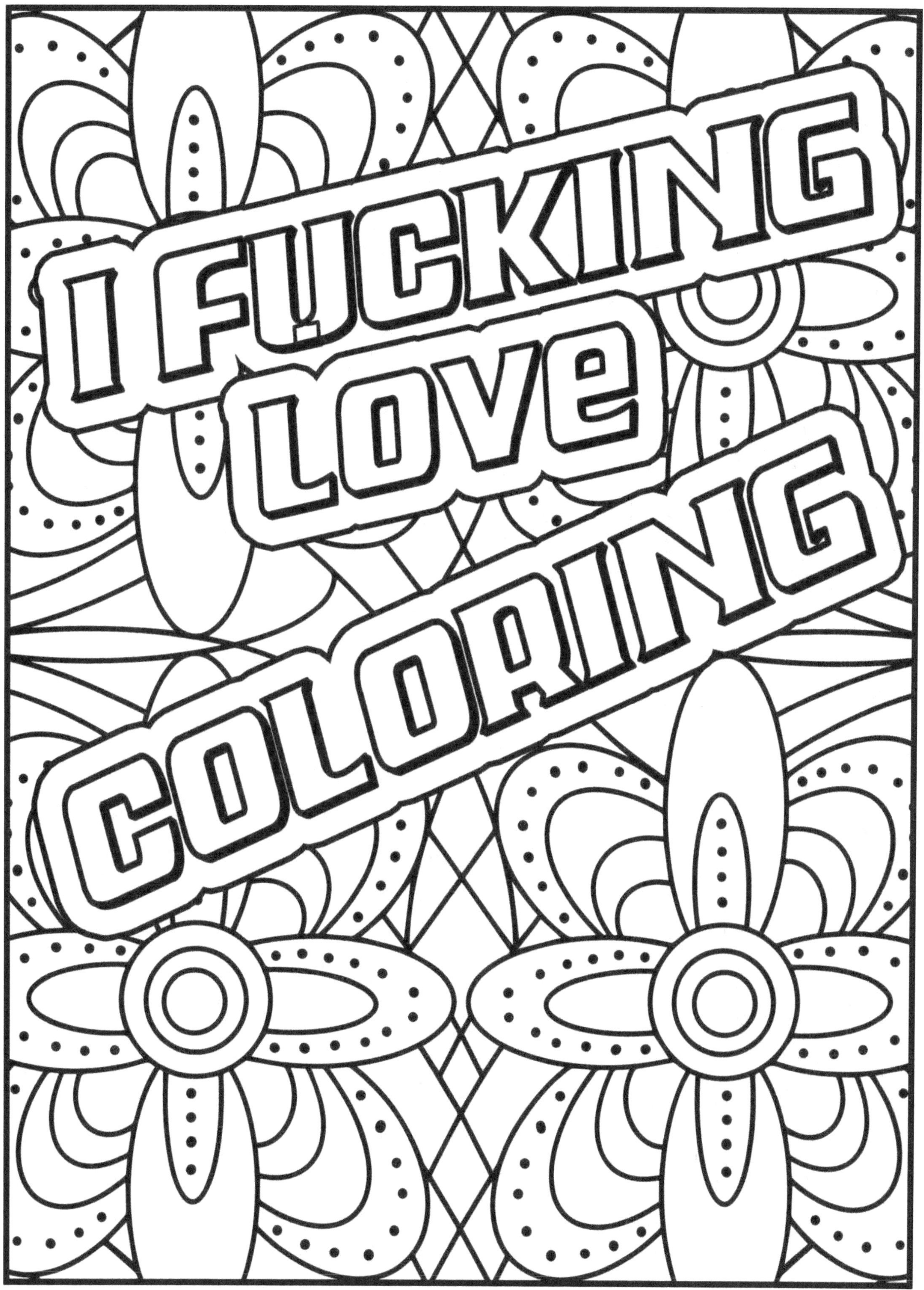

I FUCKING
LOVE
COLORING

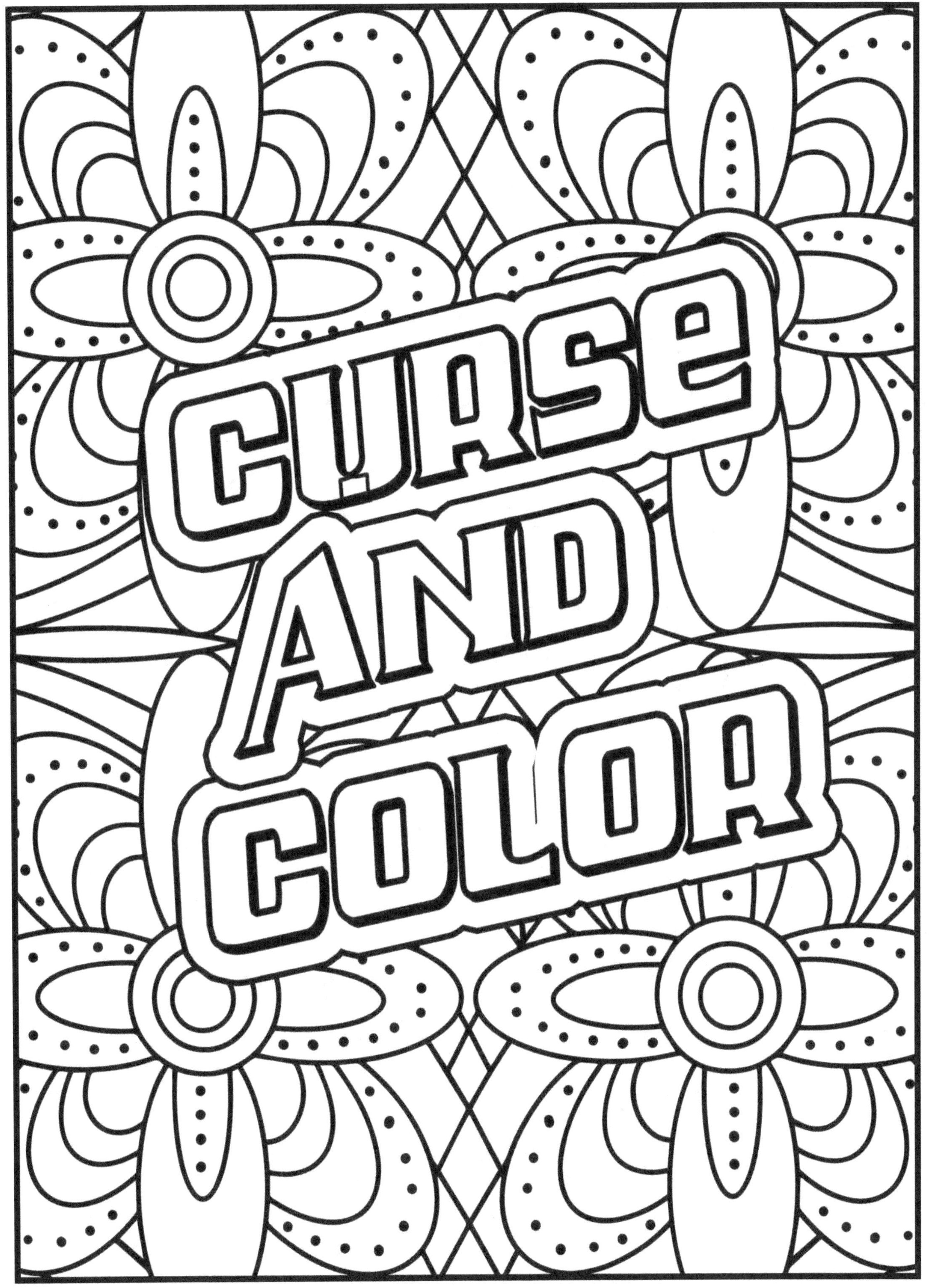

CURSE
AND
COLOR

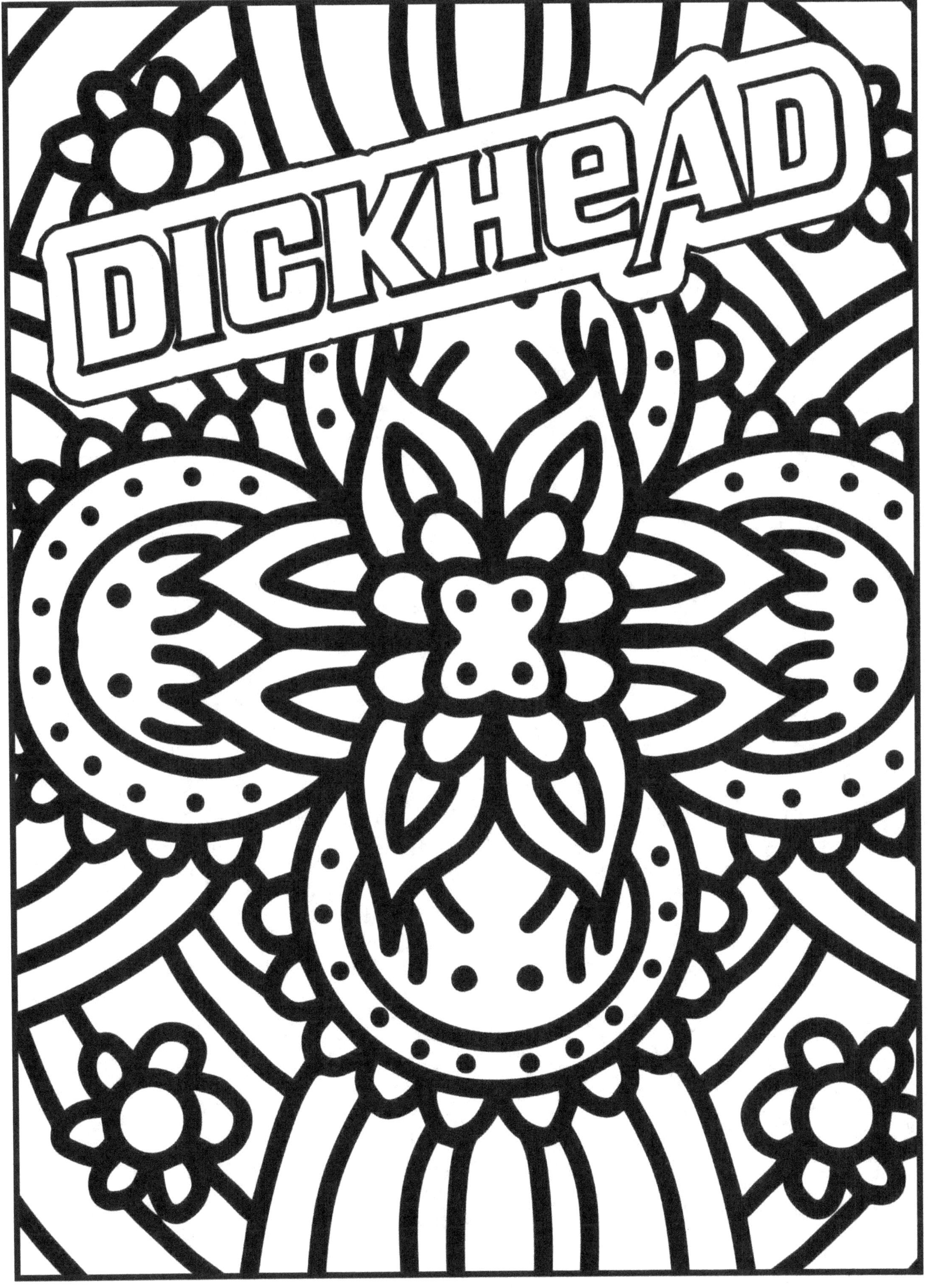

DICKHEAD

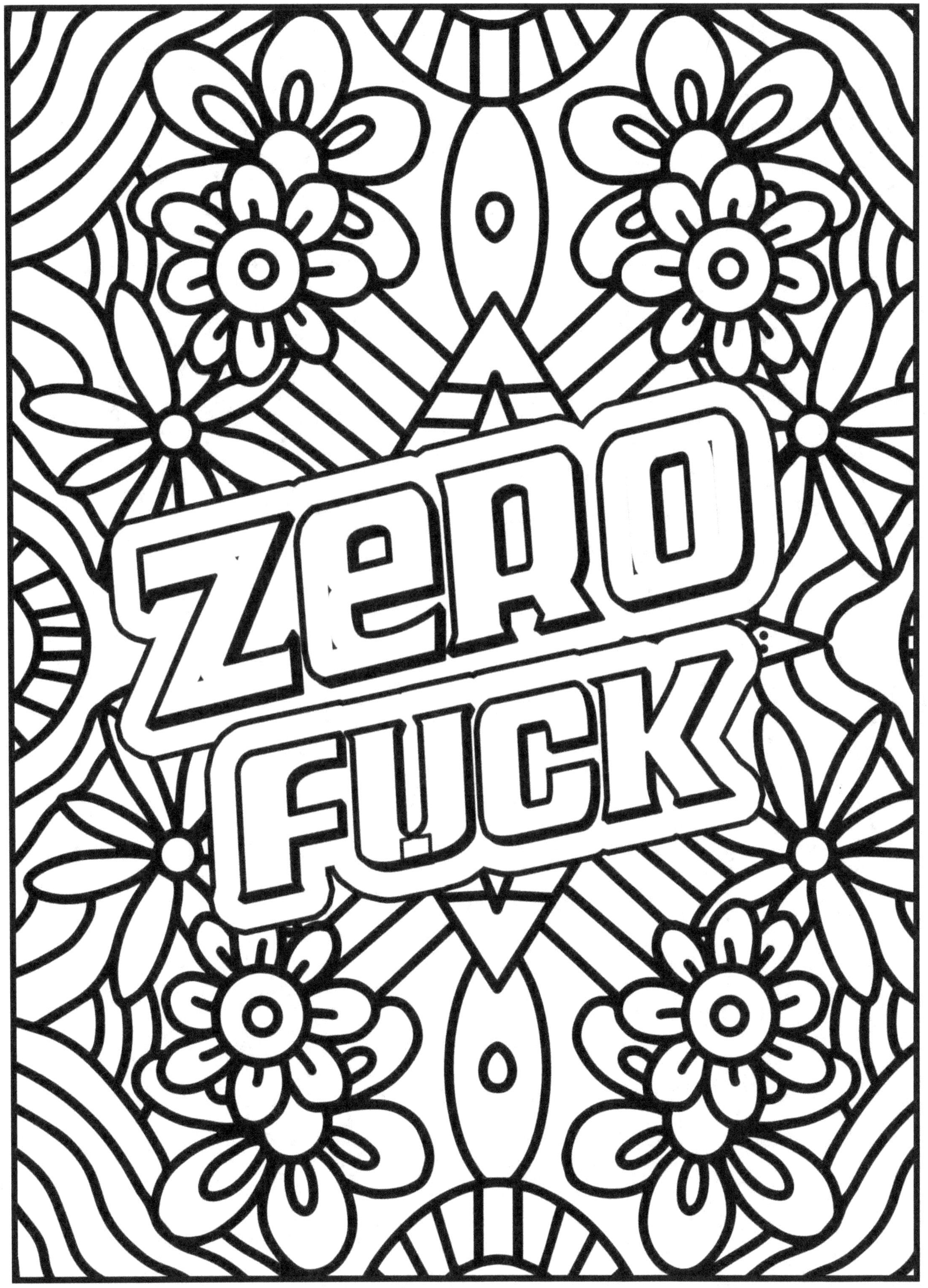

ZERO
FUCK

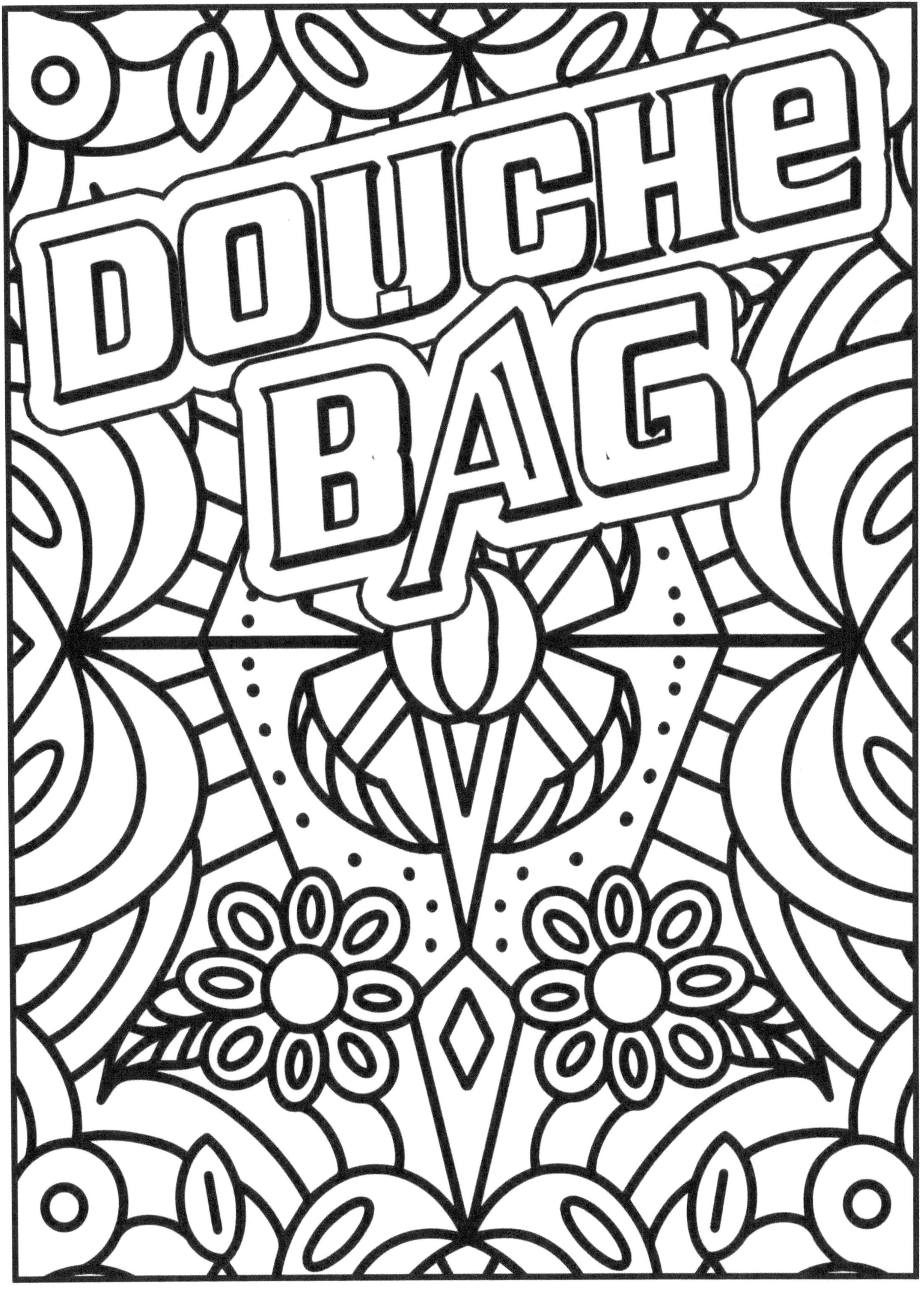

DOUCHE
BAG

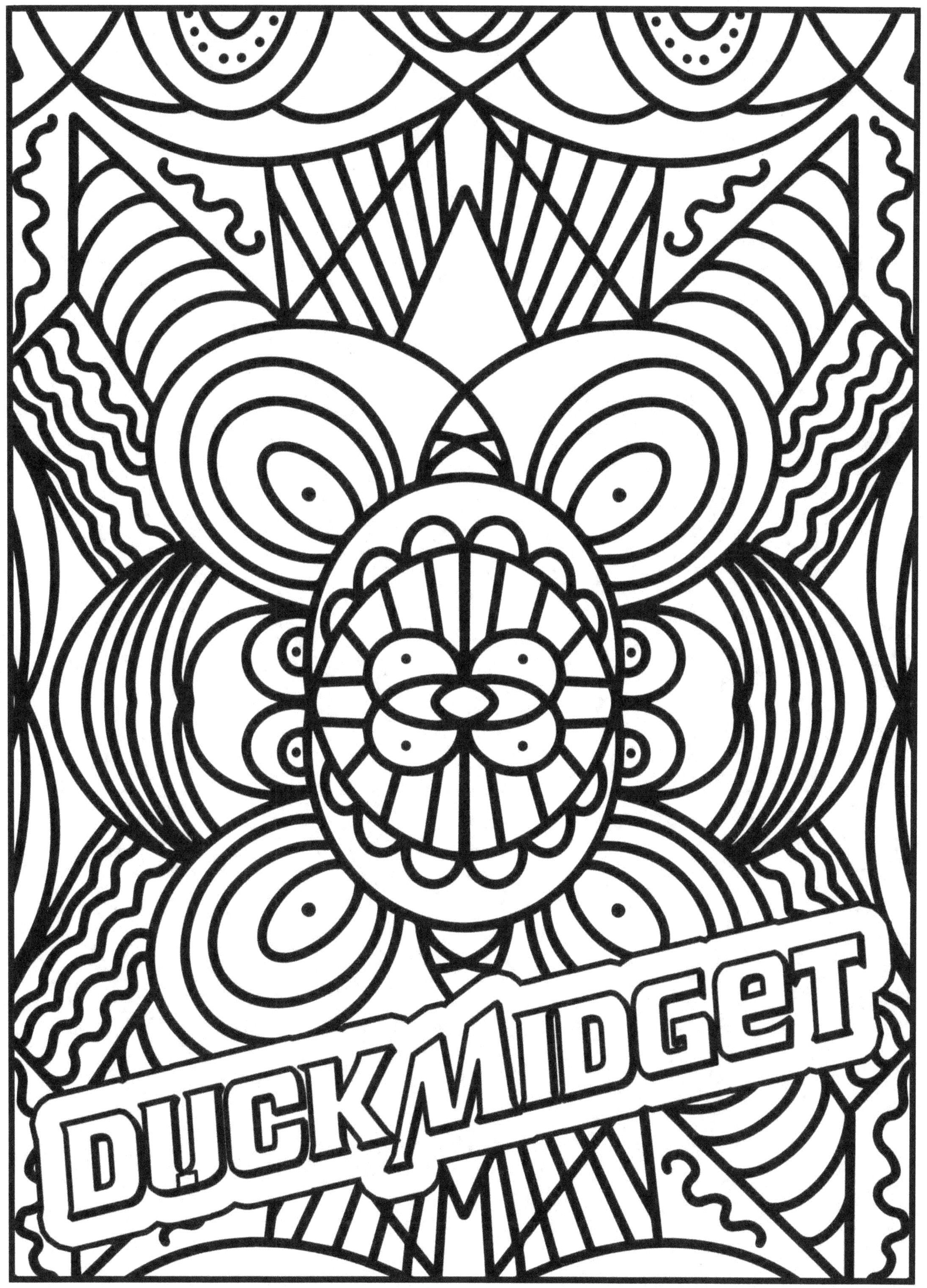

DUCKMIDGET

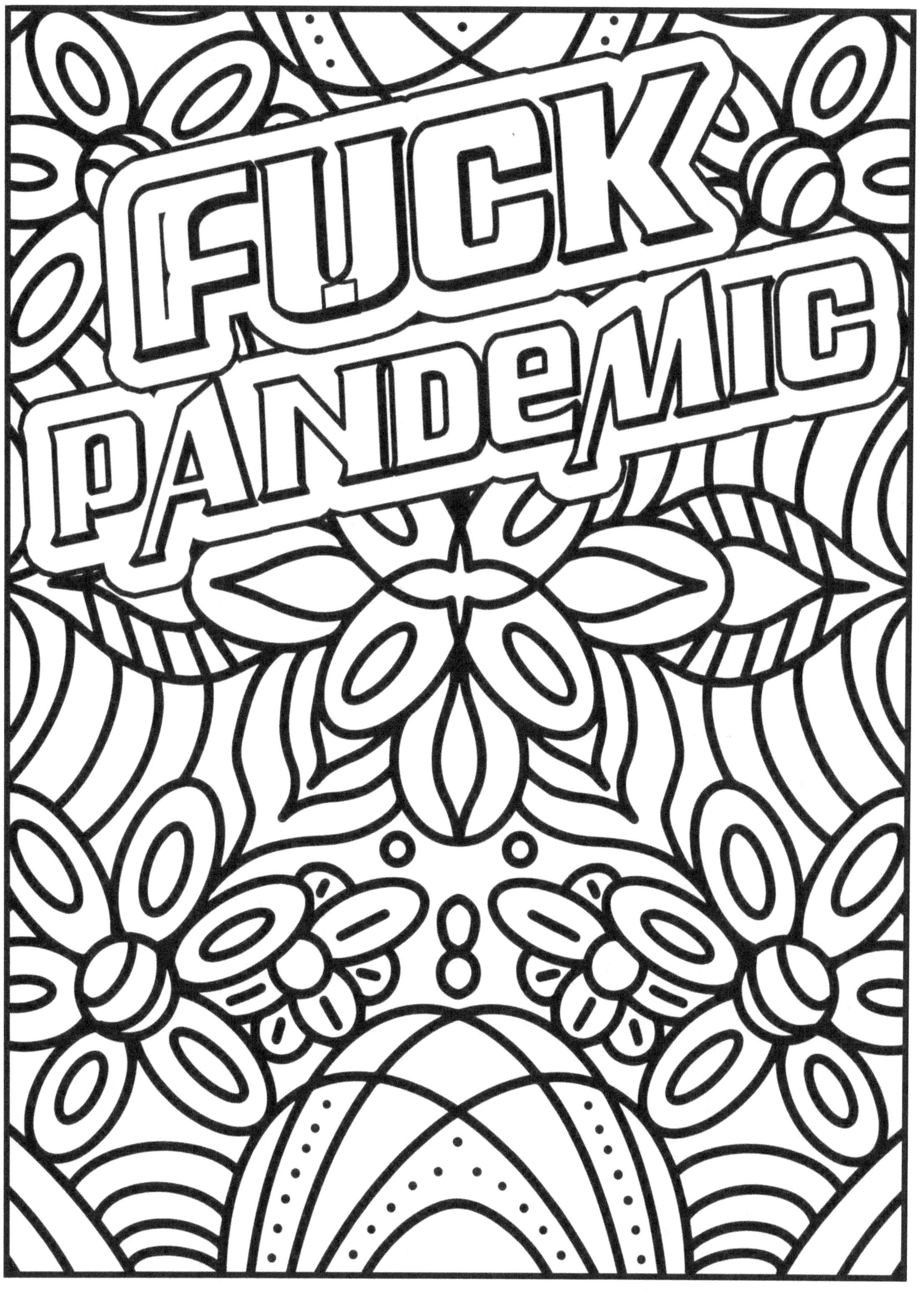

FUCK
PANDEMIC

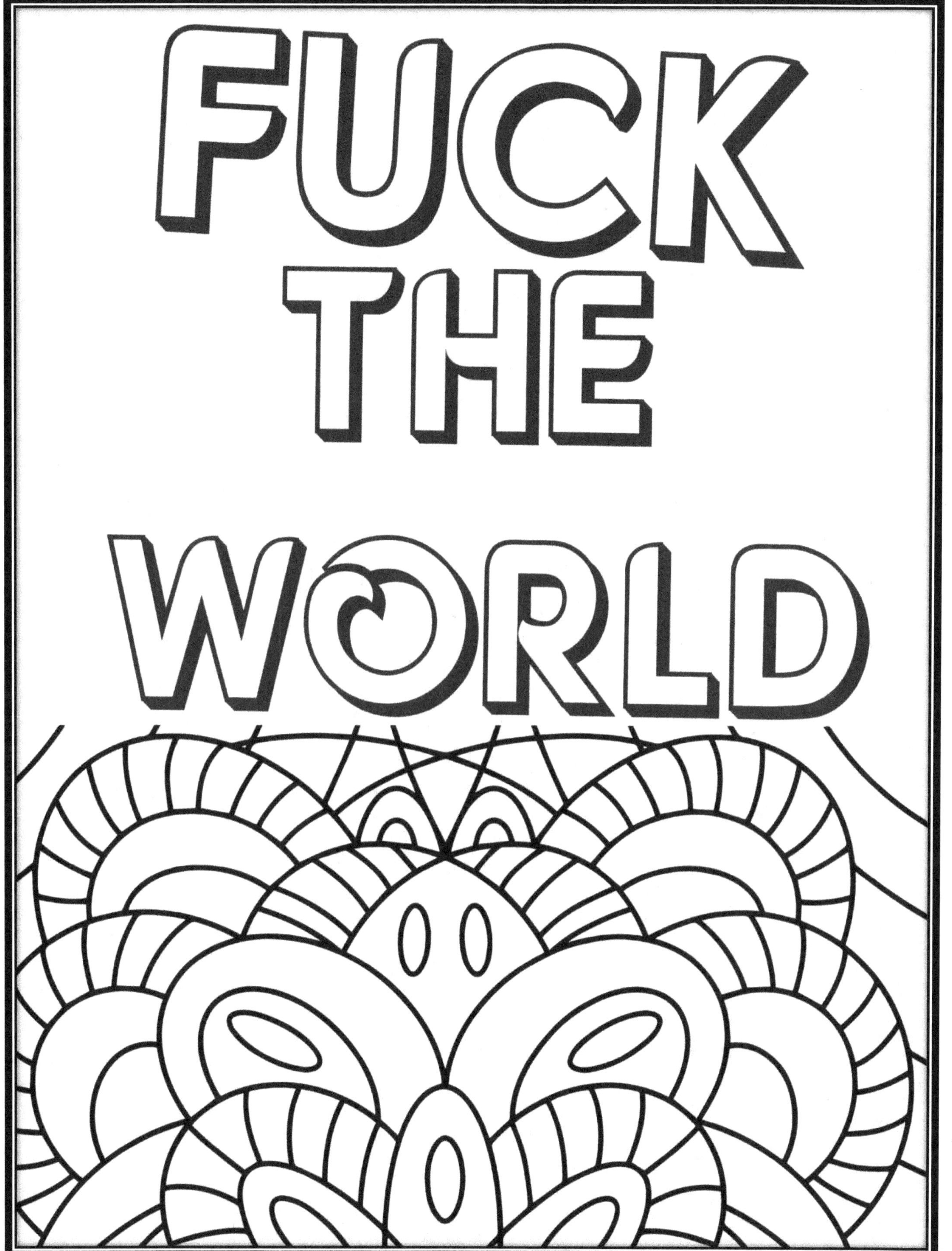

FUCK
THE
WORLD

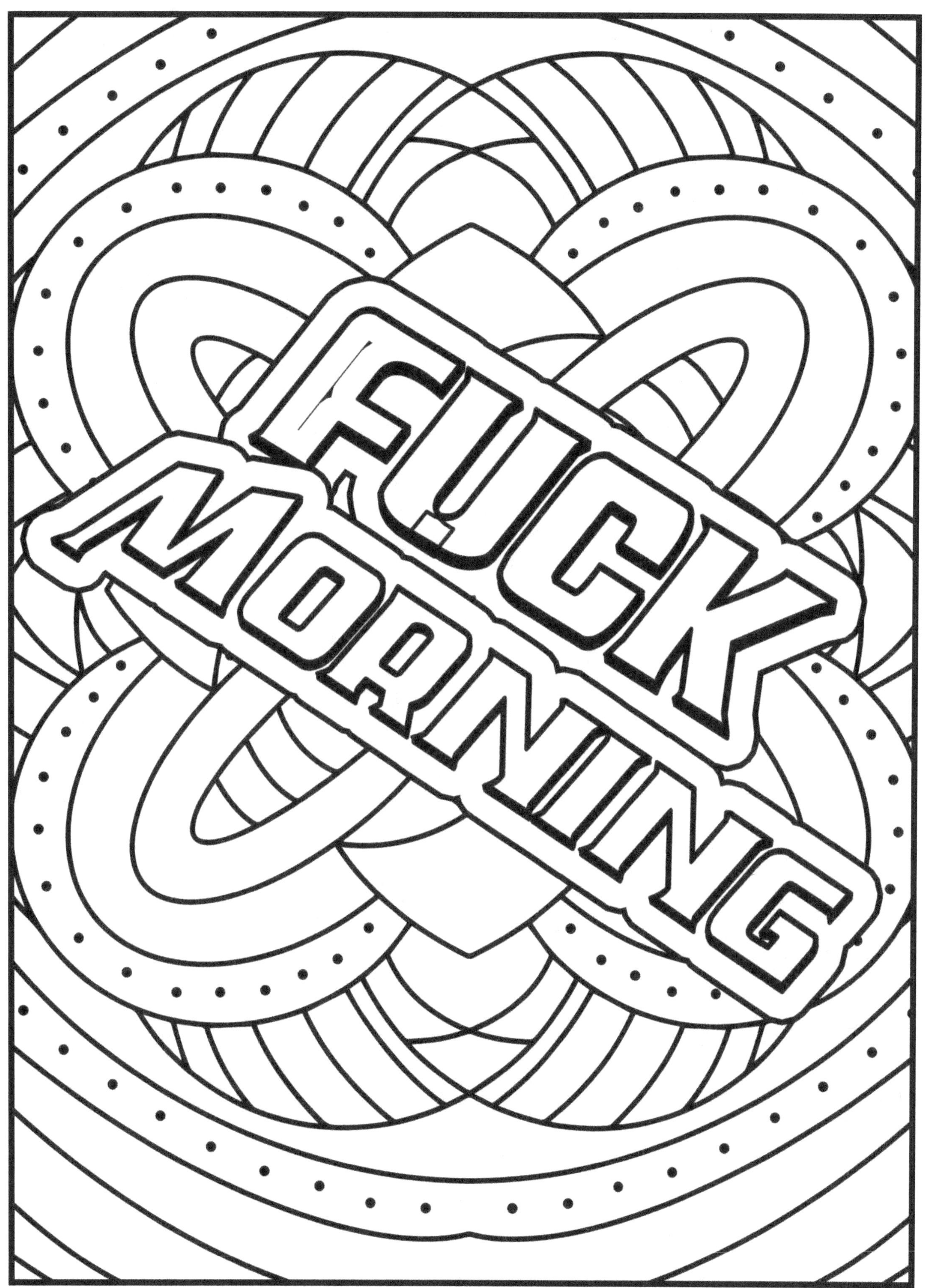

FUCK
MORNING

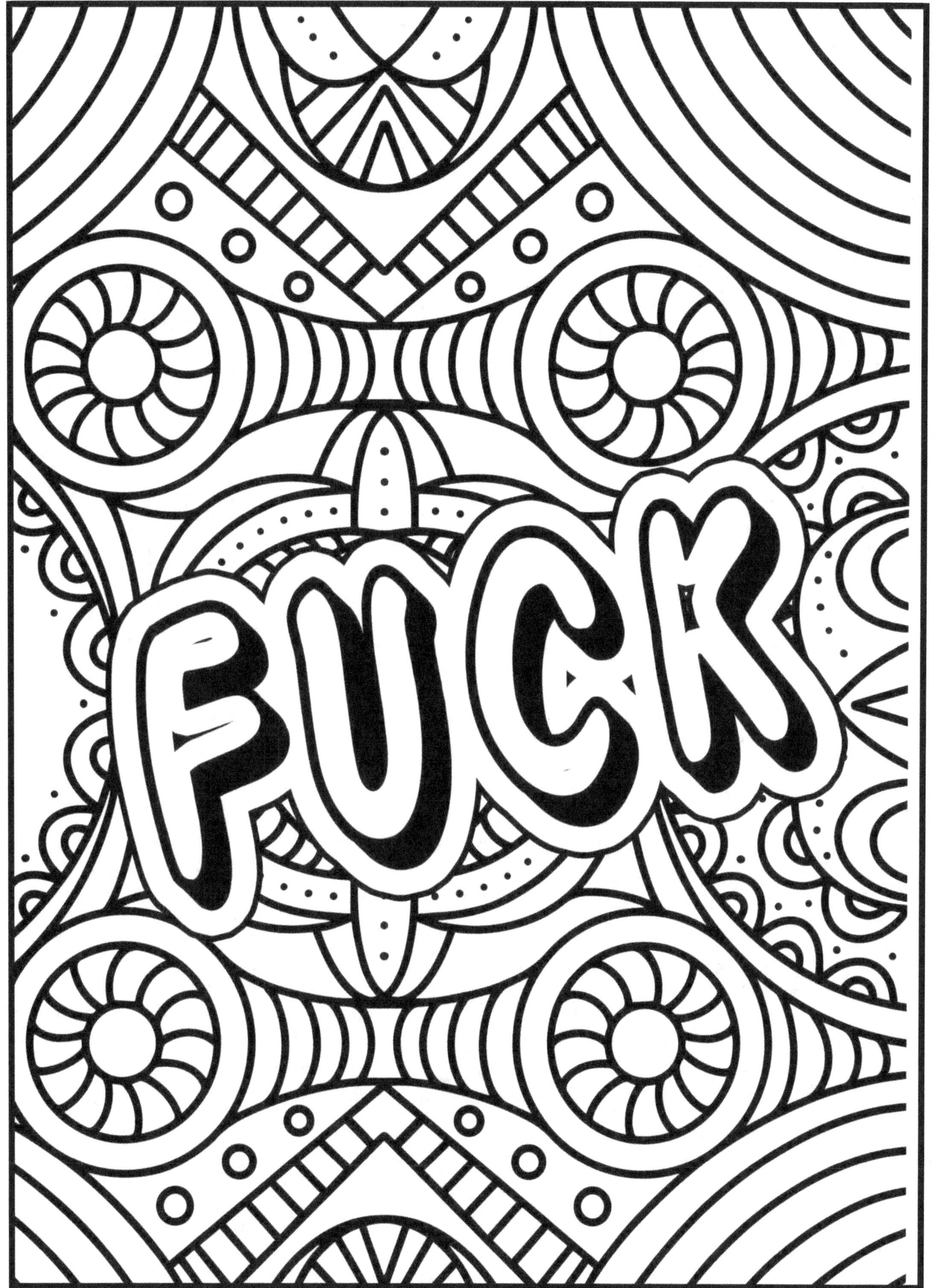
FUCK

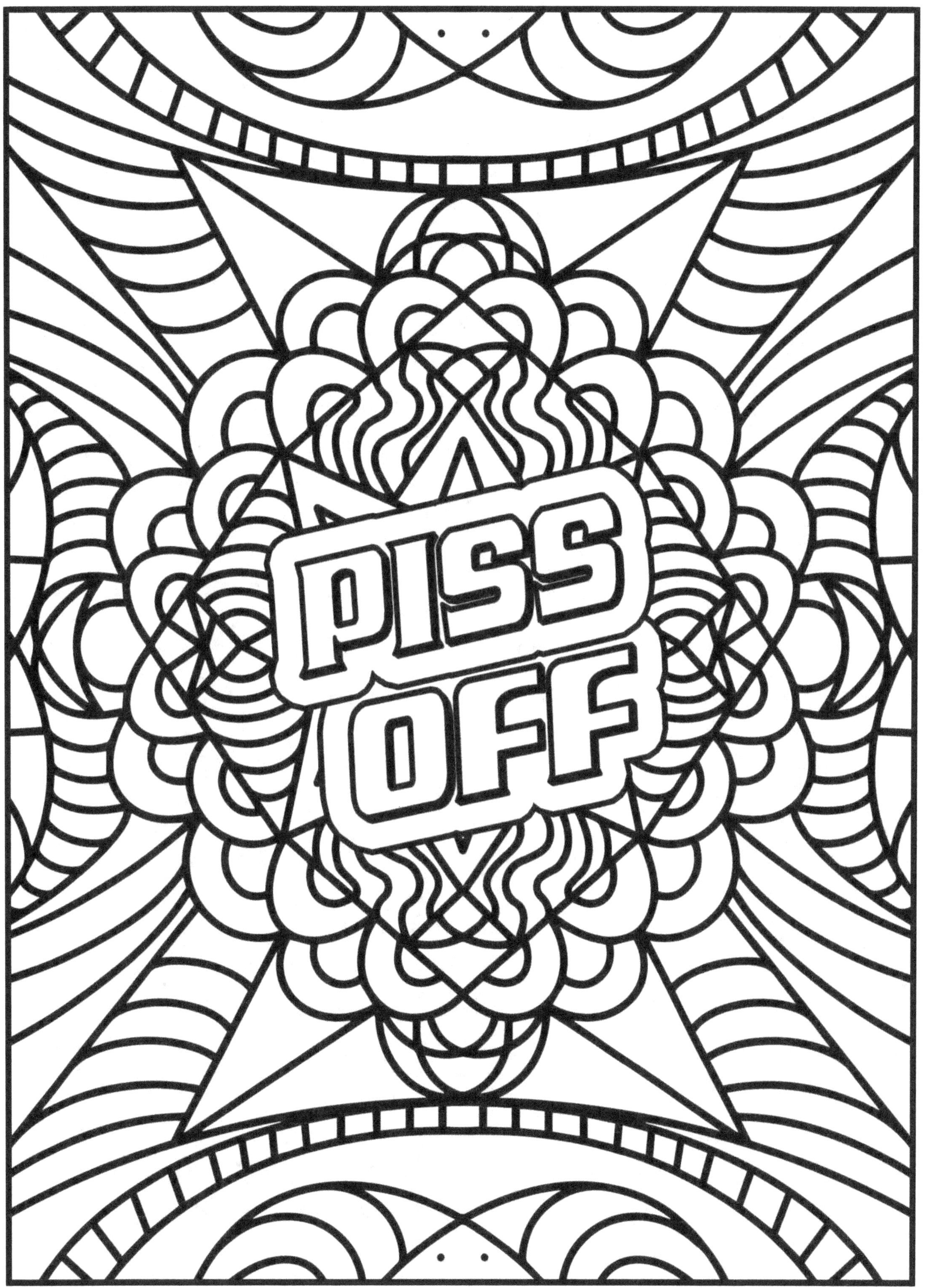
PISS
OFF

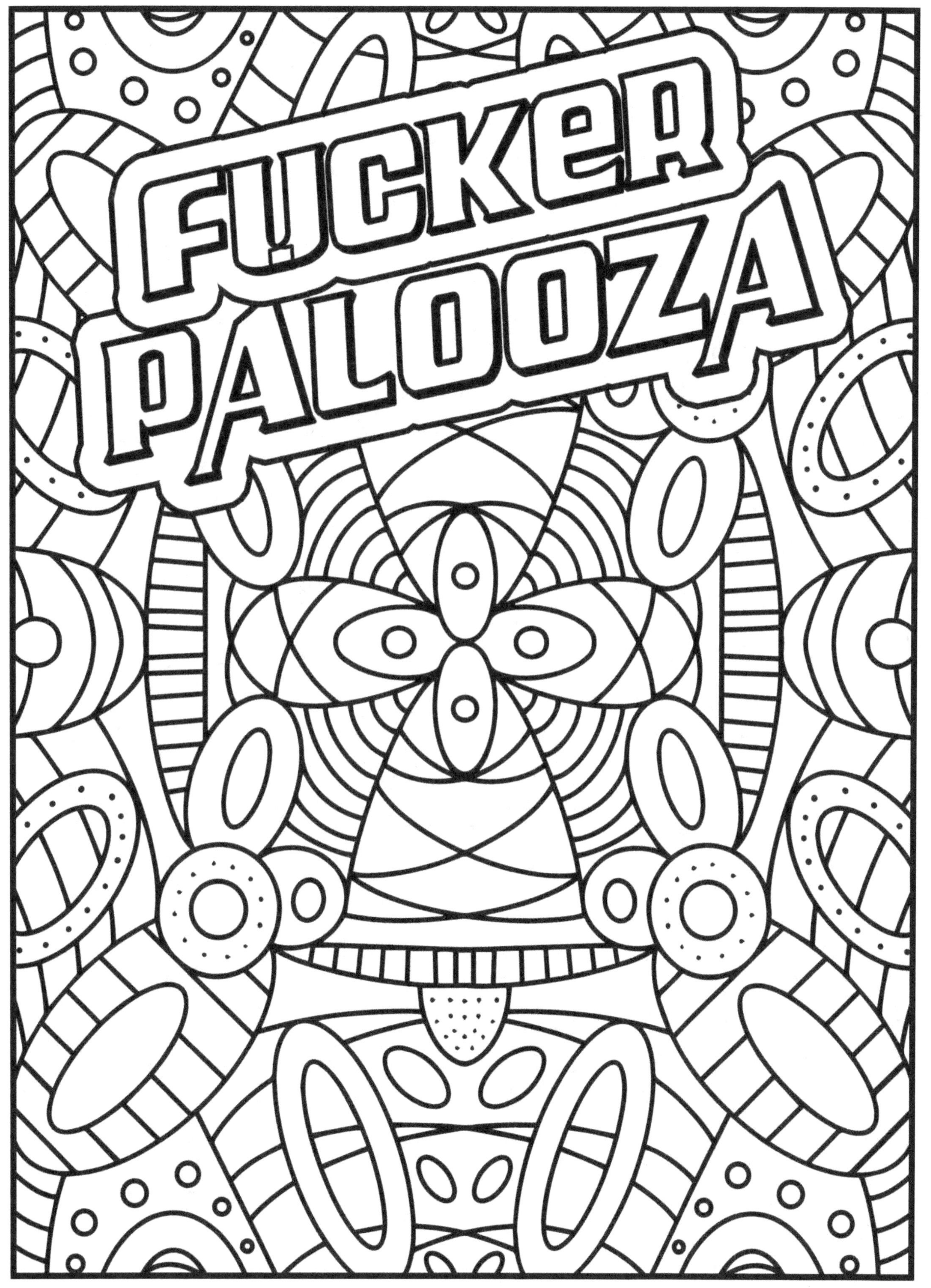
FUCKER
PALOOZA

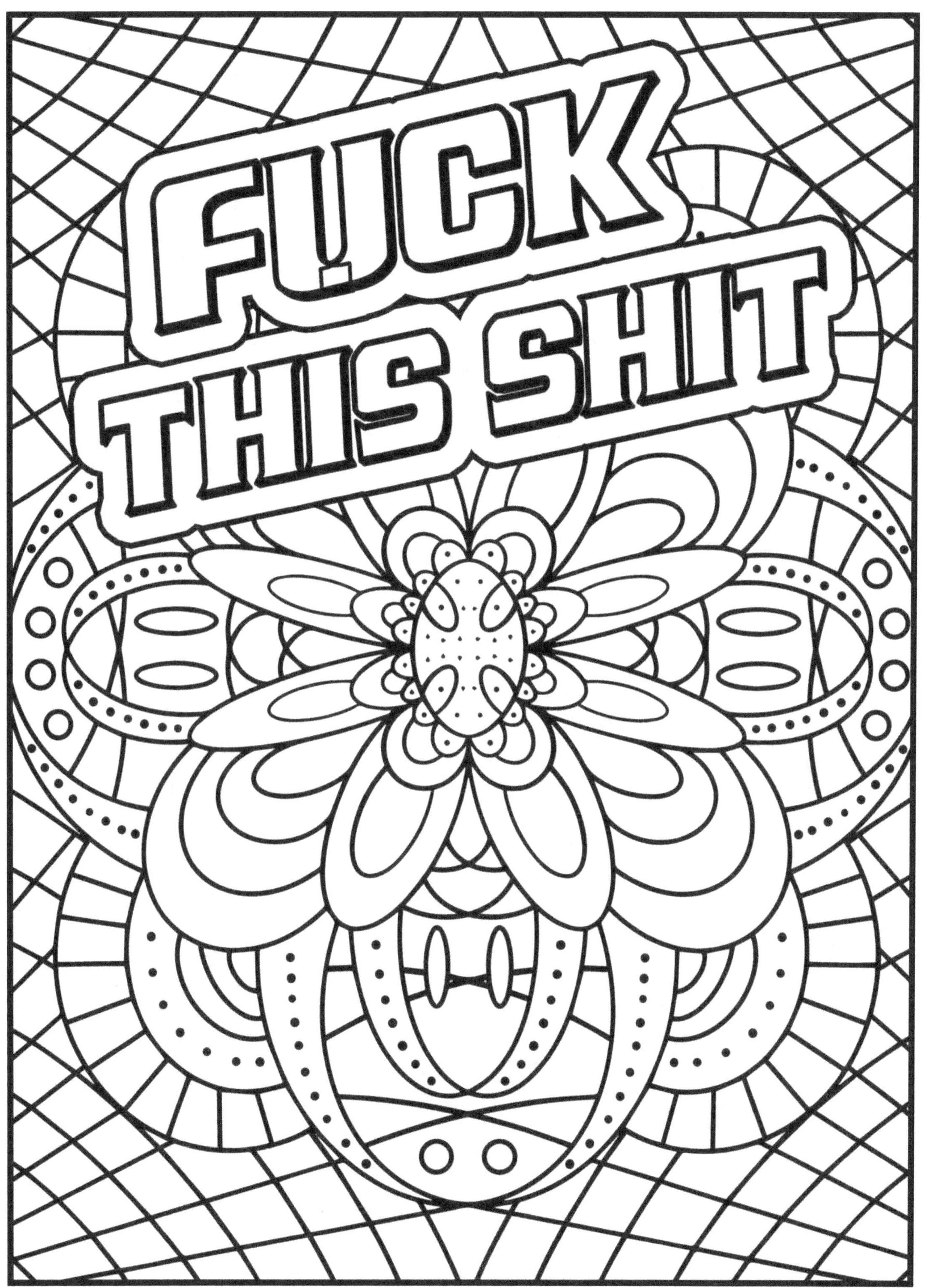

FUCK
THIS SHIT

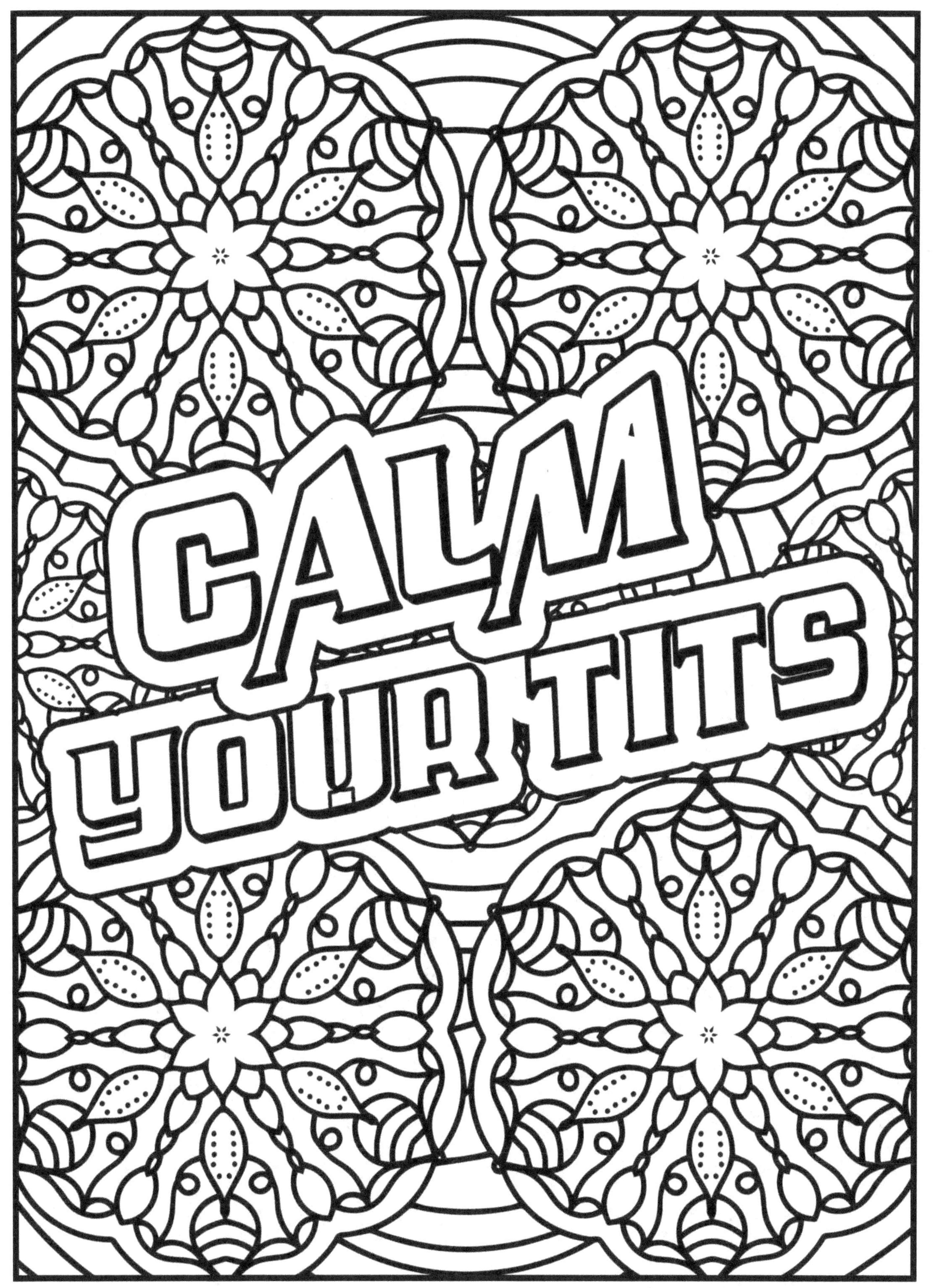

CALM
YOUR TITS

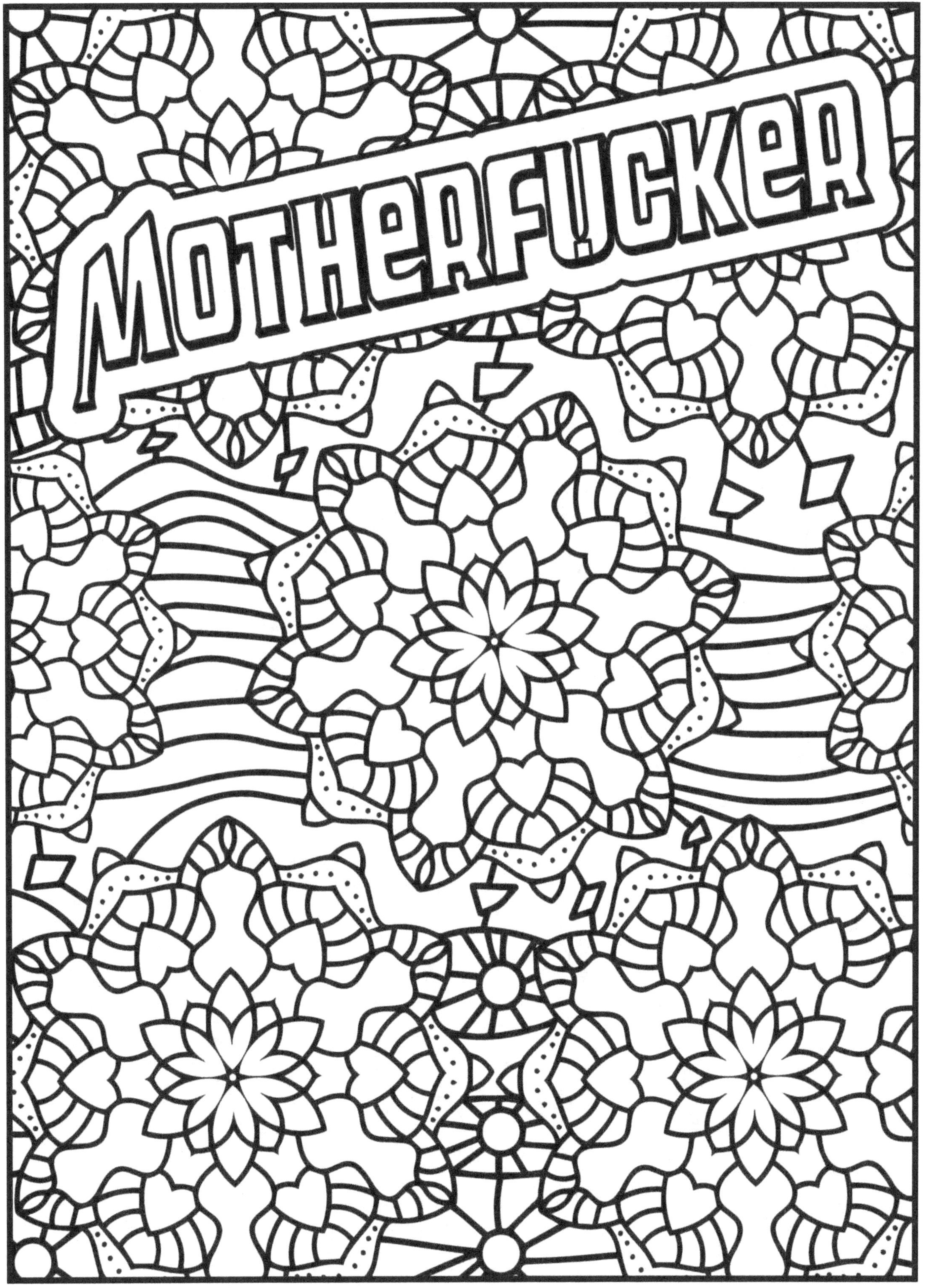

MOTHERFUCKER

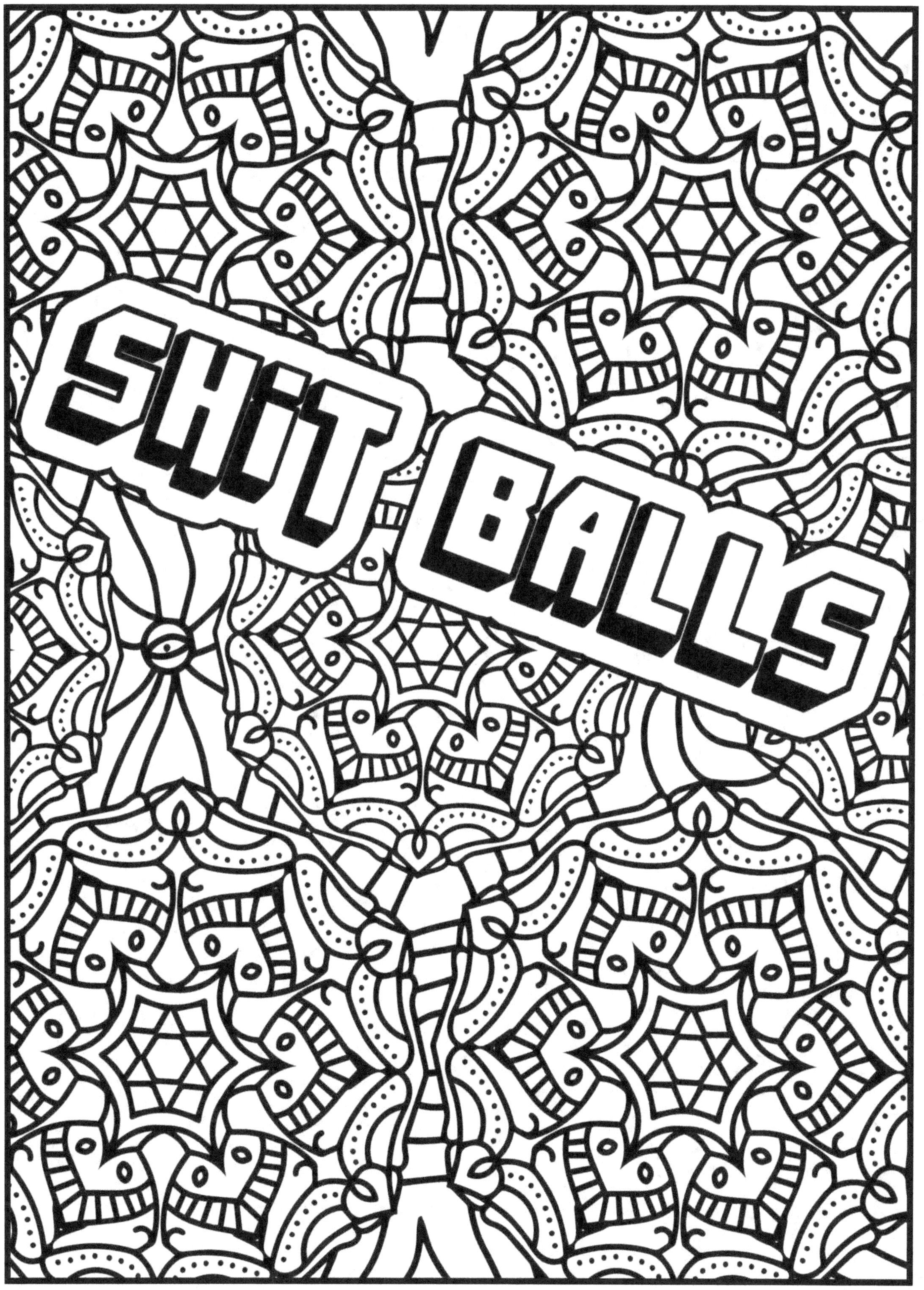
SHIT BALLS

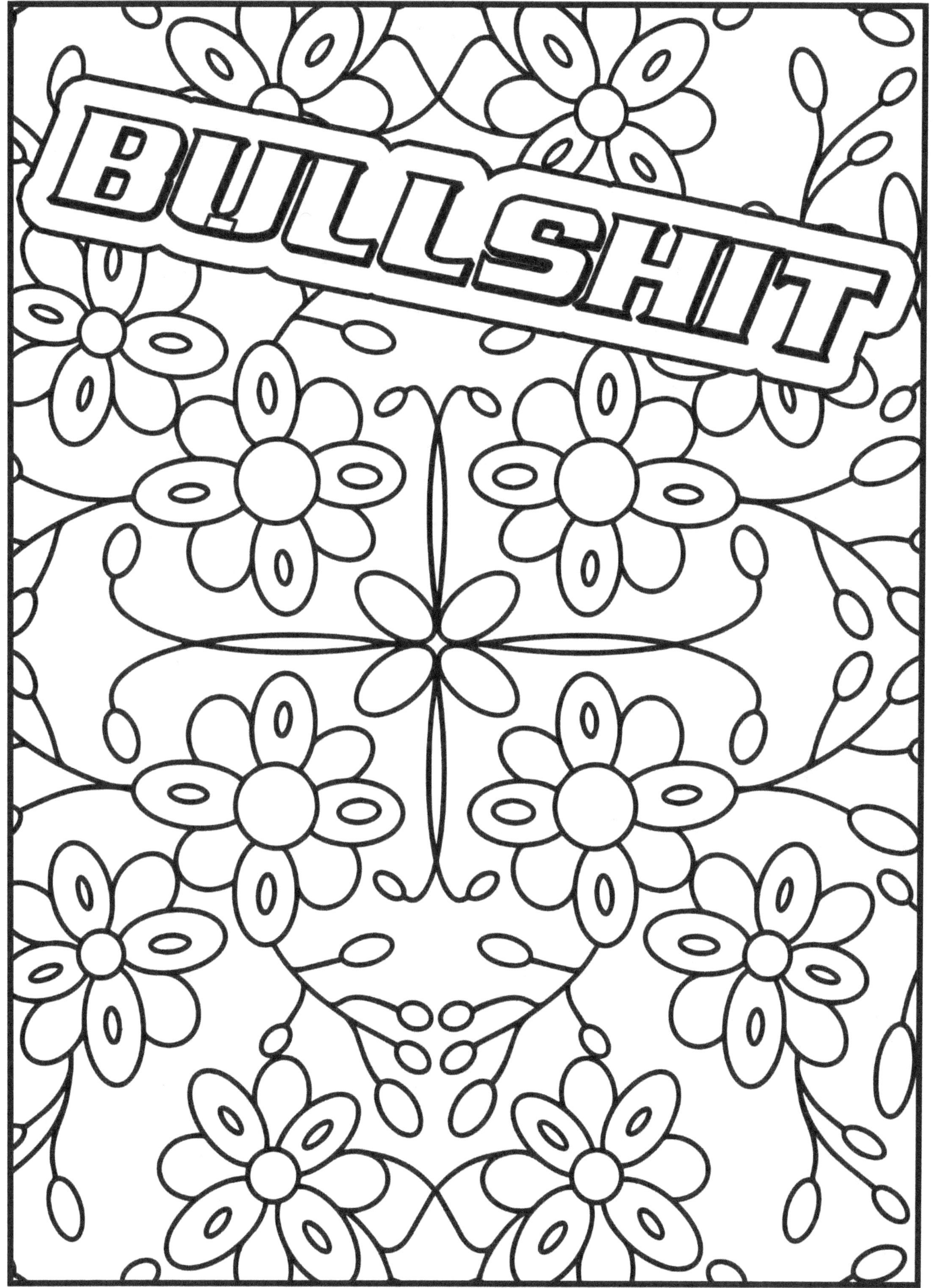
BULLSHIT

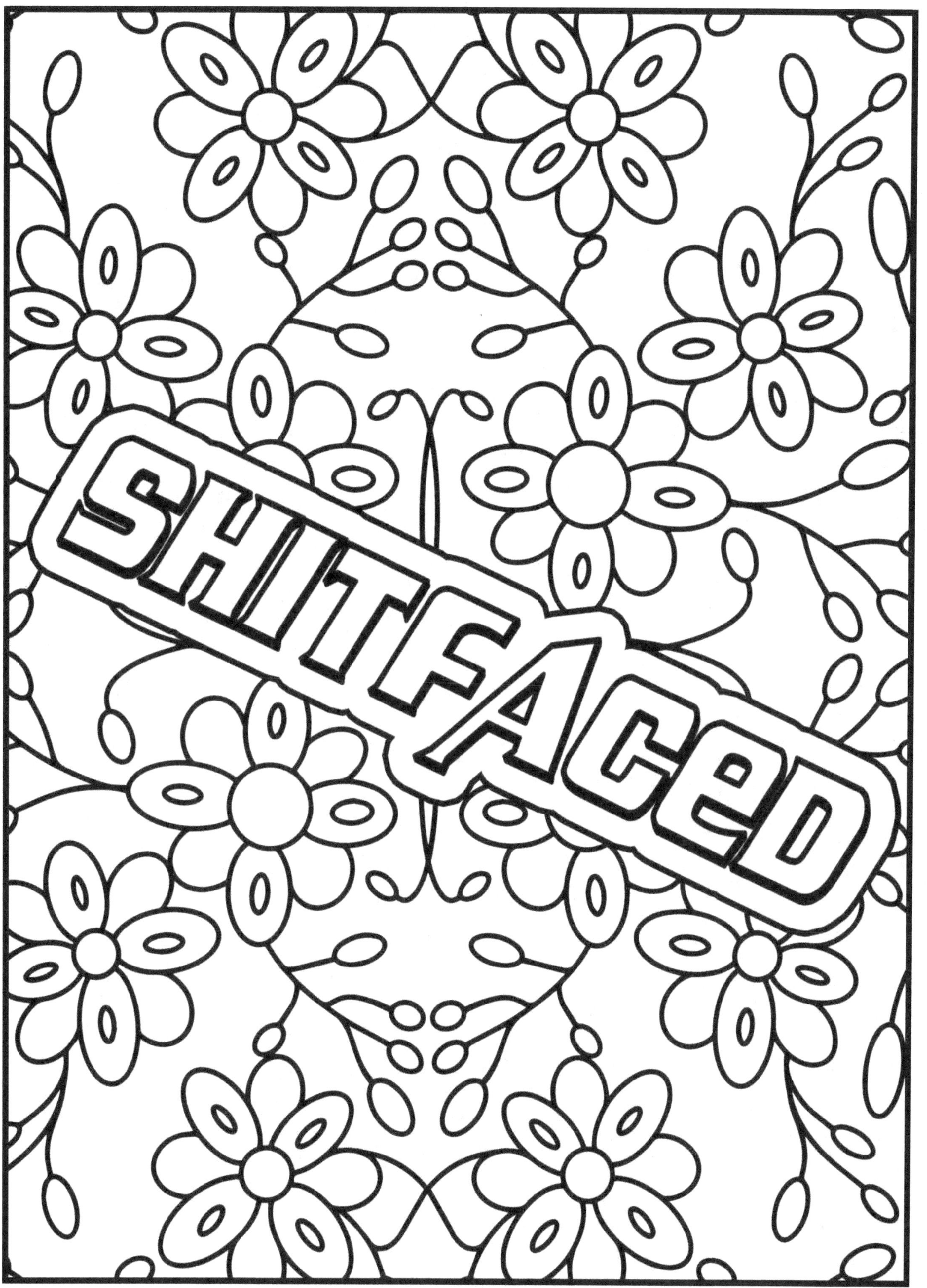
SHITFACED

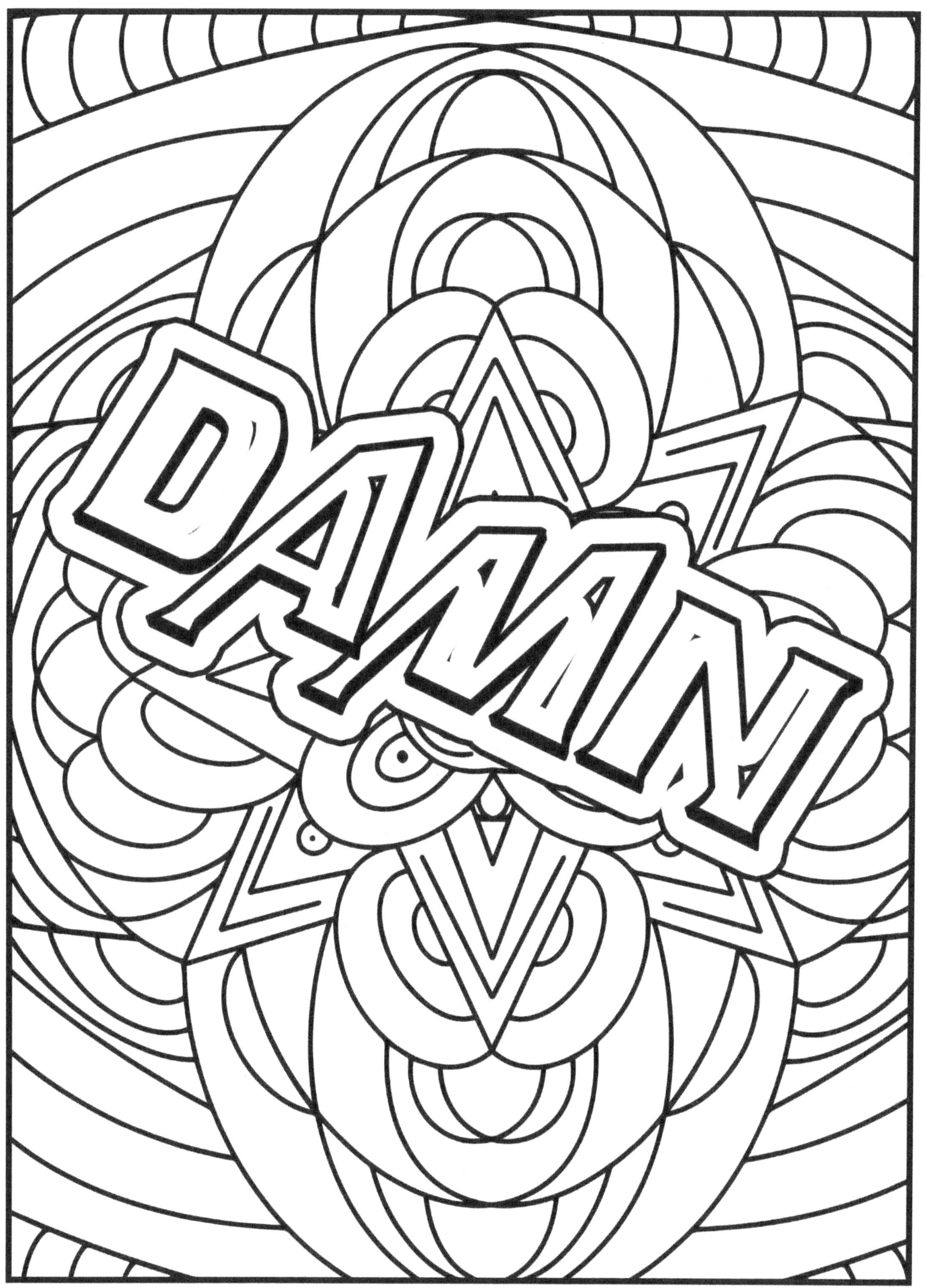
DAMN

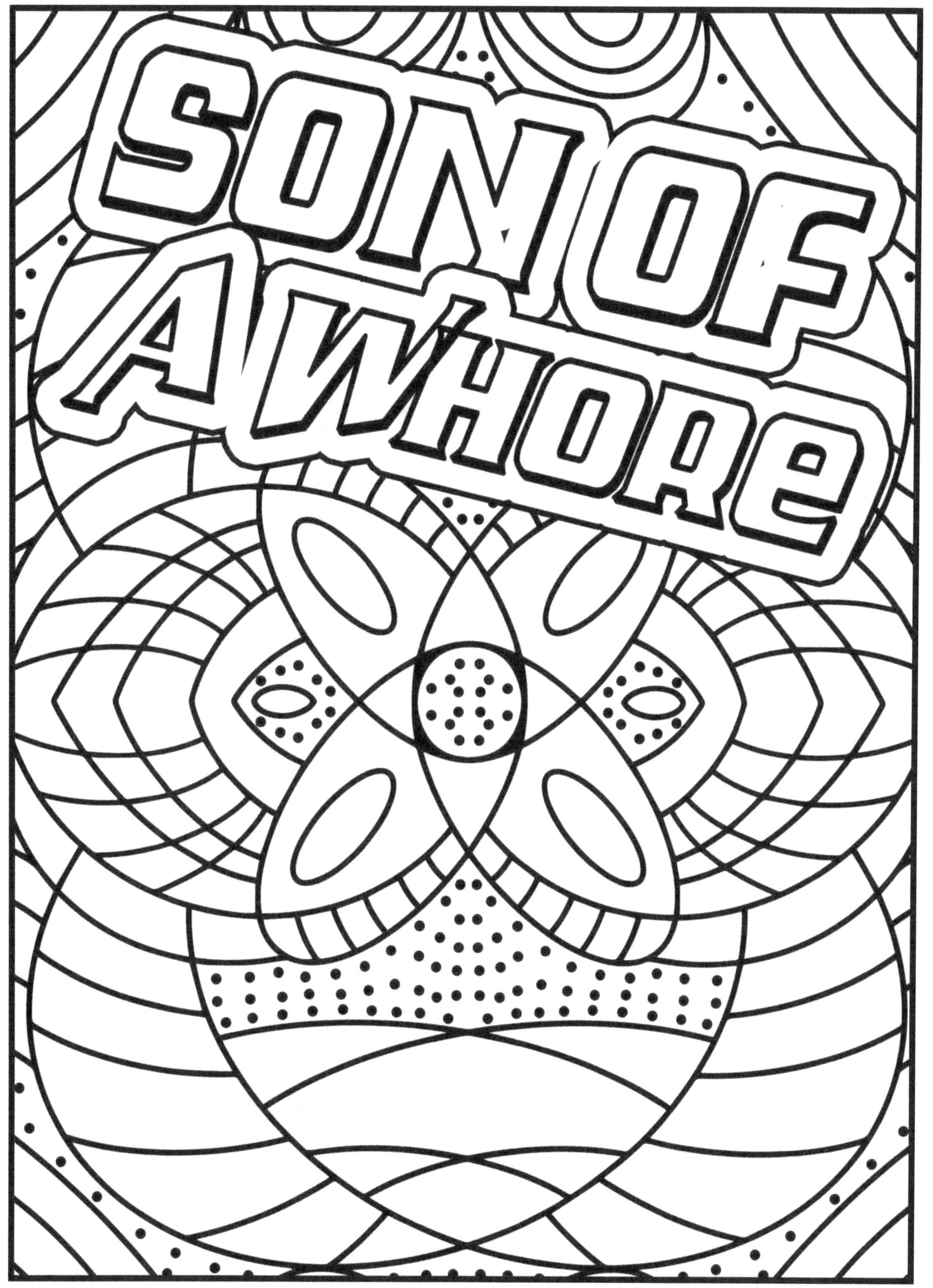

SON OF A WHORE

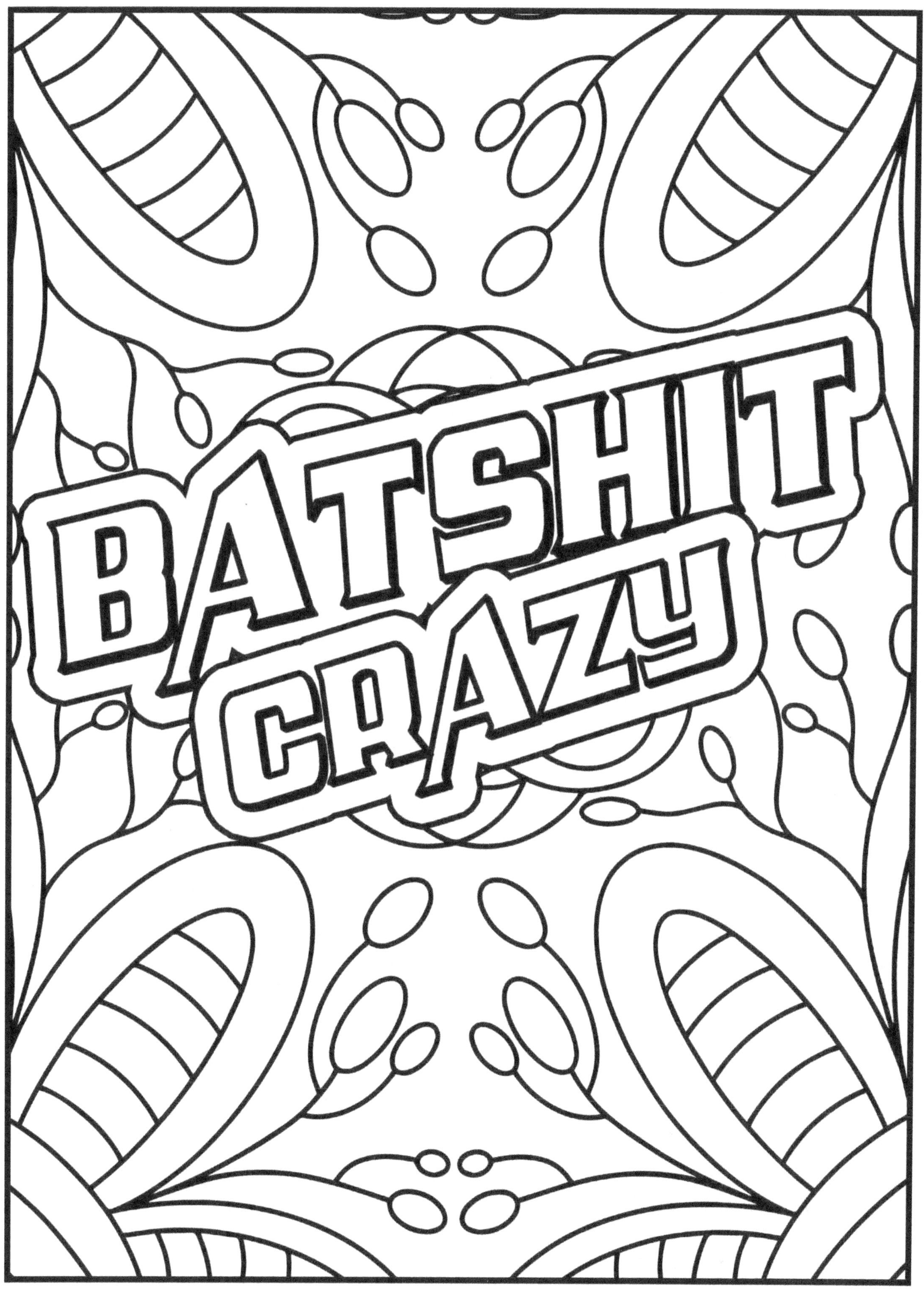

BATSHIT
CRAZY

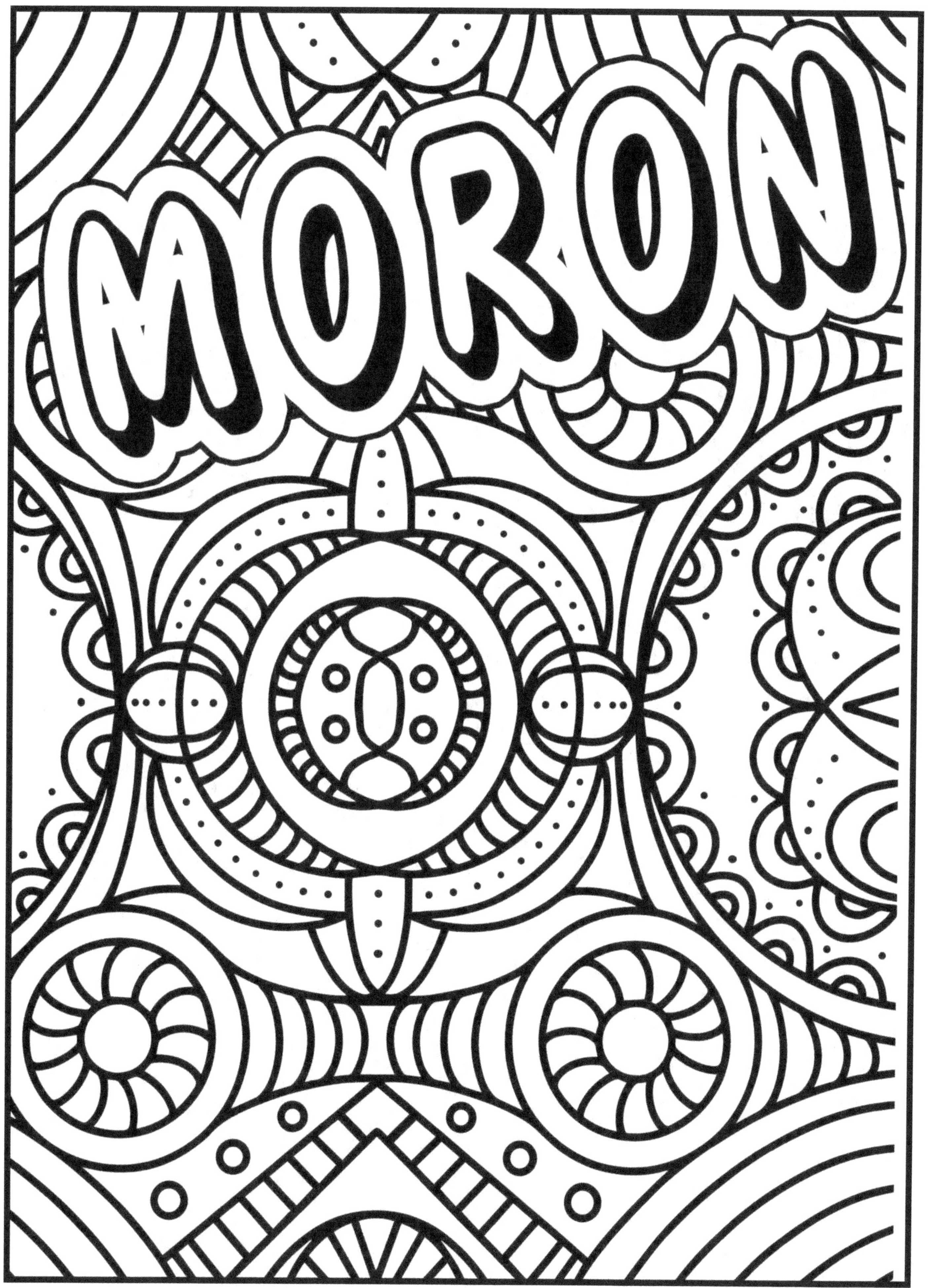

MORON

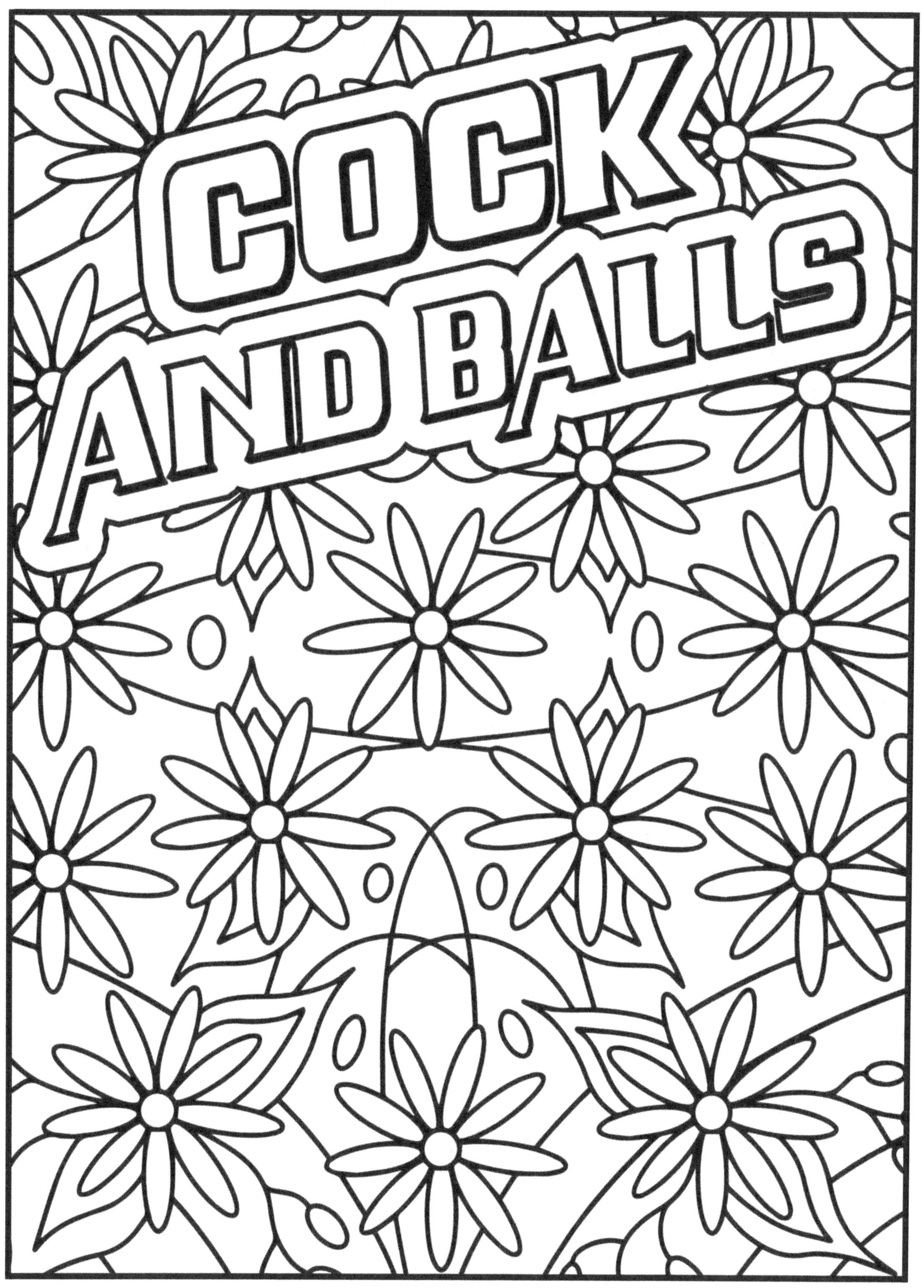

COCK AND BALLS

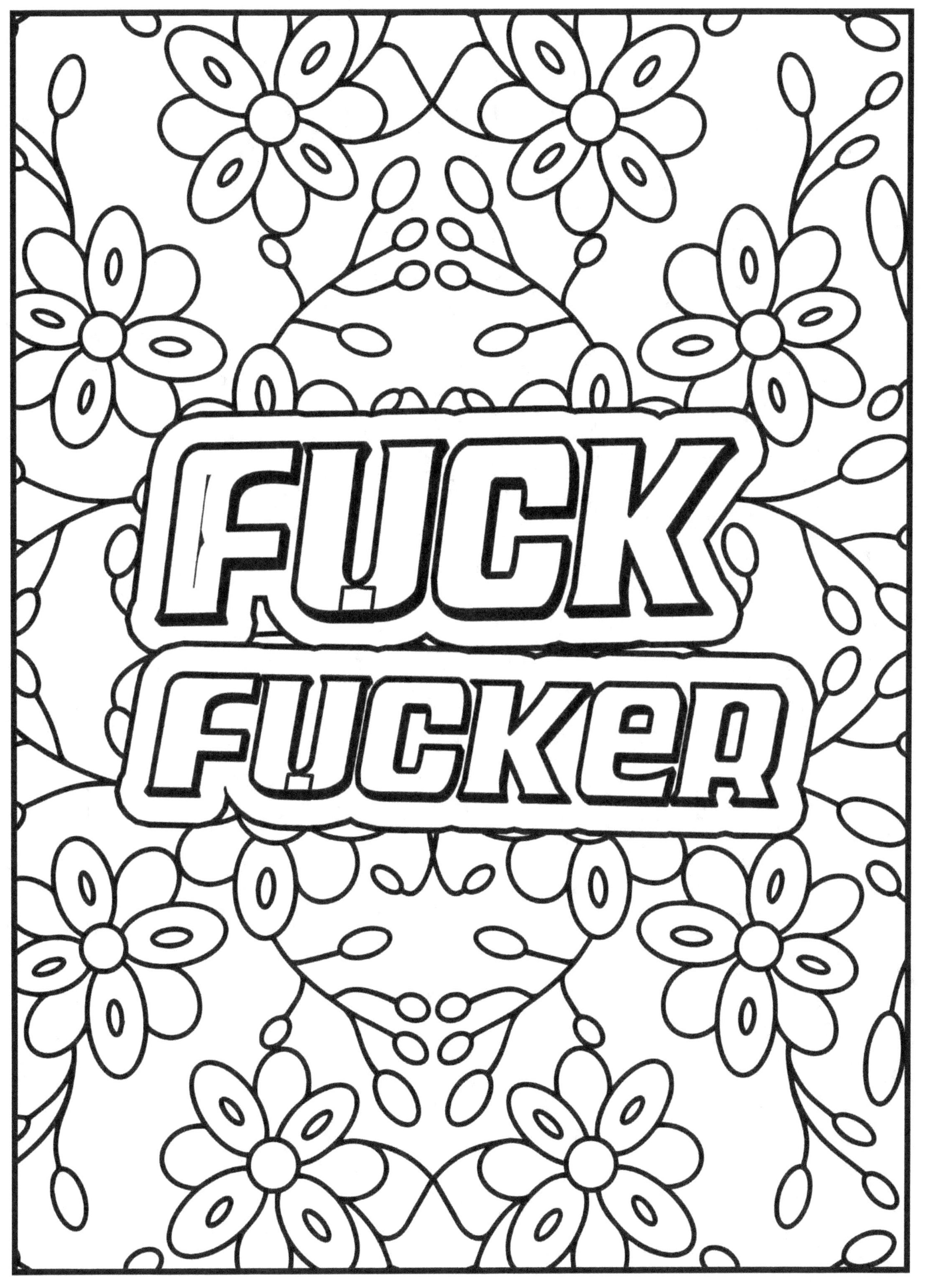

FUCK
FUCKER

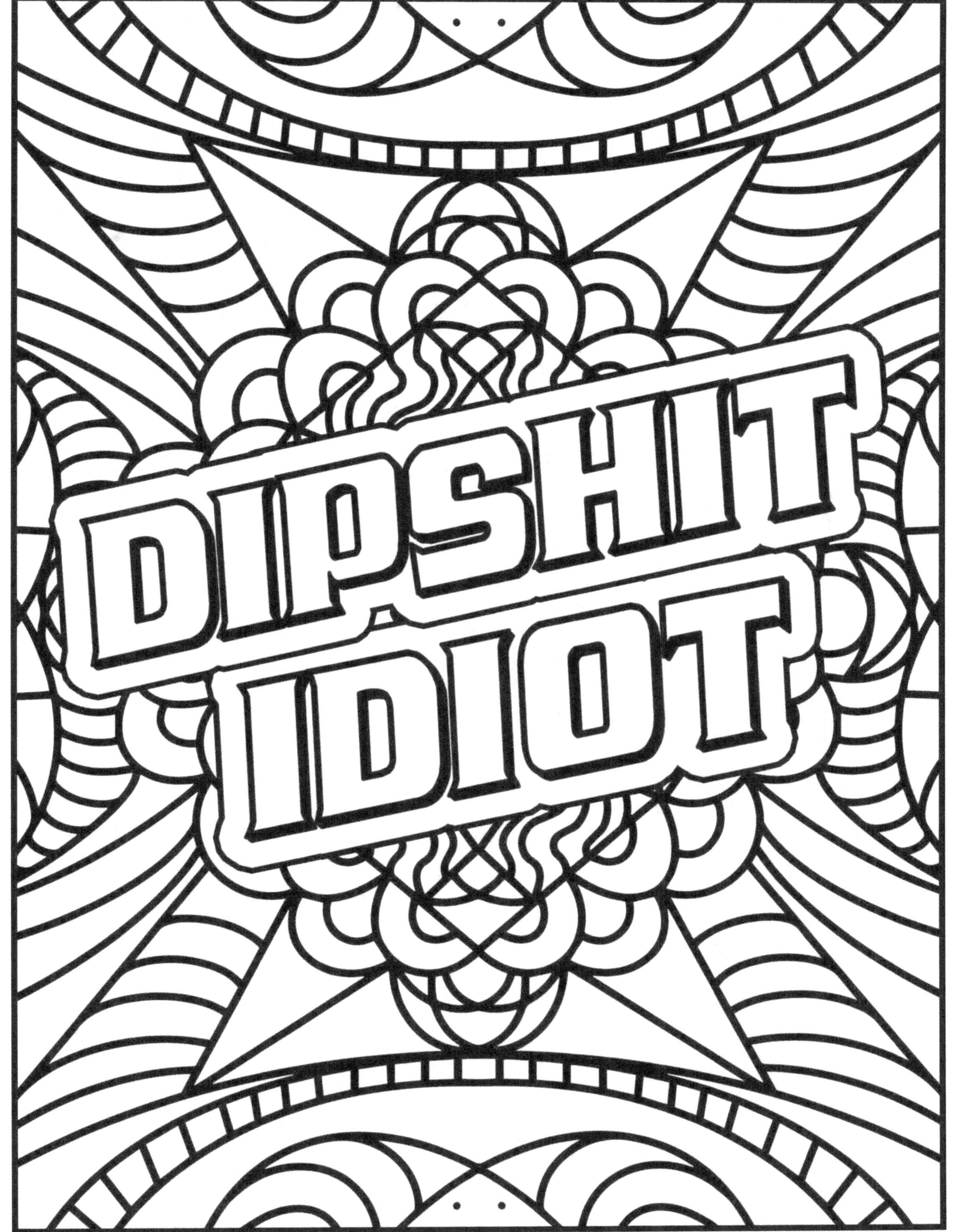
DIPSHIT
IDIOT

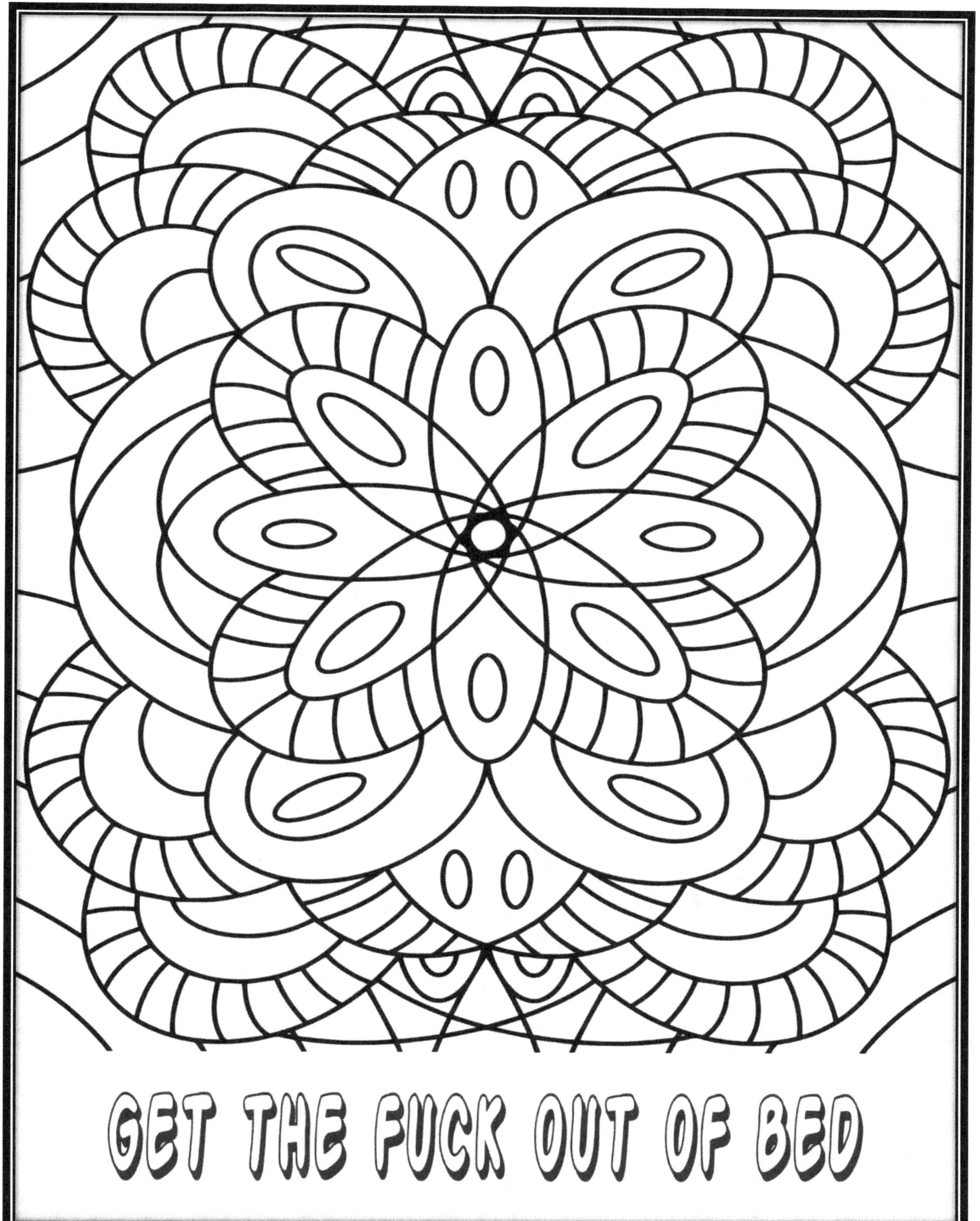

GET THE FUCK OUT OF BED

www.ingramcontent.com/pod-product-compliance
Lightning Source LLC
Chambersburg PA
CBHW082042150726
47996CB00018B/3390